THE SPLICING HANDBOOK

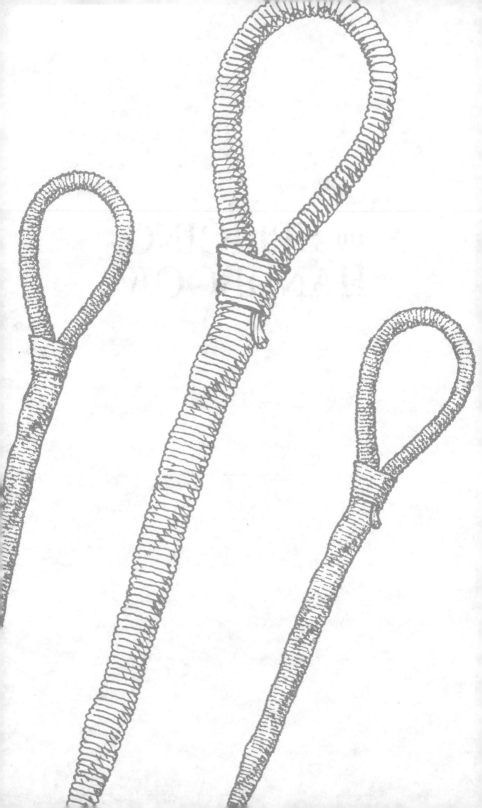

THE SPLICING HANDBOOK

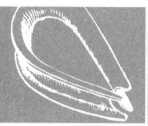
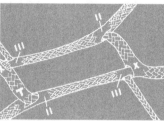

THIRD EDITION

Techniques for Traditional and Modern Ropes and Wires

Barbara Merry
with John Darwin

INTERNATIONAL MARINE/McGRAW-HILL
Camden, Maine • New York • San Francisco • Washington, D.C. • Auckland
Bogotá • Caracas • Lisbon • London • Madrid • Mexico City • Milan
Montreal • New Delhi • San Juan • Singapore • Sydney • Tokyo • Toronto

1 2 3 4 5 6 7 8 9 10 11 12 13 14 15 DOC/DOC 1 9 8 7 6 5 4 3 2 1 0
ISBN 978-0-07-173604-6
MHID 0-07-173604-2
eBook ISBN 0-07-173695-6

Library of Congress Cataloging-in-Publication Data is available from the Library of Congress.

This publication is designed to provide accurate and authoritative information in regard to the subject matter covered. It is sold with the understanding that neither the author nor the publisher is engaged in rendering legal, accounting, securities trading, or other professional services. If legal advice or other expert assistance is required, the services of a competent professional person should be sought.
—From a Declaration of Principles Jointly Adopted by a Committee of the American Bar Association and a Committee of Publishers and Association

Note: while all reasonable care has been taken in the publication of this book, the publisher takes no responsibility for the use of the methods or products described in the book.

The following chapters appeared in a slightly different form in *WoodenBoat* magazine: 20. Lizards, 21. Traditional Rope Fenders, 22. Dressing Up a Vinyl Fender, 23. Bow Puddings, 24. Baggywrinkle, 25. A Cargo Net.

McGraw-Hill books are available at special quantity discounts to use as premiums and sales promotions or for use in instructional or group programs. To contact a representative, please e-mail us at bulksales@mcgraw-hill.com.

This book is printed on acid-free paper.

Questions regarding the content of this book should be addressed to www.internationalmarine.com

Questions regarding the ordering of this book should be addressed to
The McGraw-Hill Companies
Customer Service Department
P.O. Box 547
Blacklick, OH 43004
Retail customers: 1-800-262-4729
Bookstores: 1-800-722-4726

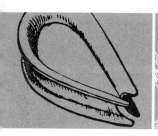
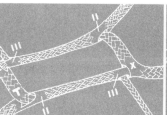

CONTENTS

PART TWO

SPLICING WIRE ROPE

PART THREE

ROPEWORK PROJECTS

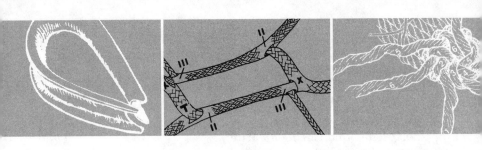

ACKNOWLEDGMENTS
TO THE THIRD EDITION

Thanks to: The good folks at Trawlworks, Narragansett, Rhode Island, especially Jim and Peter for their lessons and advice on wire;

Bob Dollar, LCDR USN Retired;

Andrew Boyko, for his knowledge of the Mill Valley Splice; and,

Brennan Hale, Master Rigger, West Marine, Middletown, Rhode Island.

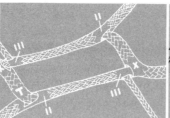

PREFACE
TO THE THIRD EDITION

Since 1987, when it was first published, mariners around the world have turned to *The Splicing Handbook* while learning and perfecting the art of joining line and other nautical rope-craft. The third edition reflects the growth of my own repertoire of skills over the years. Organized in three parts for the first time, this expanded edition of *The Splicing Handbook* offers splicing guidance and instruction for both synthetic and wire rope.

- Part One, Splicing and Seizing Modern Ropes, includes all the rope projects featured in the earlier editions of this book.
- Part Two, Splicing Wire Rope, is an all-new wire section, featuring background information, an introduction to wire types and care, and five splicing projects.
- Part Three, Ropework Projects, highlights five new and fabulous ropework activities with which to expand your skills.

At *WoodenBoat* magazine's nineteenth annual WoodenBoat Show (June 2010) I stopped by Jeff Pearson's Antique Tools & More booth. As I admired the antique wooden, two-foot hinged rulers he often has available for purchase—my choice for measuring lengths of rope—my eyes fell upon a small booklet on wire splicing. I couldn't get my hands on it fast enough, nor could I pay for it fast enough. Ten dollars was all Jeff wanted for it. I would have paid more!

As I handed over my money, Jeff commented, "I'm surprised this is still here." I was pleased to hear him say that, because it confirmed my belief that wire splicing information and instruction are indeed in demand. In demand, yes—but not new.

In Part Two, I present age-old wire techniques in modern language and drawings. My advice to students learning the art of splicing is like my advice to those learning to tie knots. I advise knotting students to find the knot in question in other sources, like *Ashley's Book of Knots* or *The Marlinspike Sailor* or *Knots and Splices*—there are several. Then, as you learn new knots, refer to all the sources to find your way.

Likewise, if you're just learning to splice wire, study the information in this book, find other sources, observe the work of a master rigger (I have even been known to pay for lessons!), and then reexamine the information here to hone your skills.

Acquiring the wire-splicing and ropecrafting skills outlined in this book will reward you time and again, both in your mastery of these skills and in the safe and efficient operation of your vessel.

PART ONE

SPLICING
AND SEIZING
MODERN ROPES

ONE

Introduction to Splicing

Rope in use is attached to something else—to another rope, to an object to be moved or prevented from moving, or to an object that prevents the rope from moving. The attachment can be accomplished with a knot, but knots are bulky and, by their nature, cut the breaking strength of the rope in half. The alternative is a splice, which is capable of attaining a rope's full strength.

Splicing teaches you not only about the splice itself, but also about the construction and quality of the raw material. The knowledge gained from practicing the splices in this handbook should enable you to splice *any* general-purpose rope. But remember the wise advice, as true today as it ever has been: "Measure twice, cut once."

No single splicing technique can work on all rope because the constructions vary considerably. Rope designers, who are functional artists much like architects, seek a perfect construction using the characteristics of various fibers: strengths, abrasion resistance, weight, shrinkage, and elasticity. They must consider resistance to heat, cold, sunlight, chemicals, water, dye, and microorganisms, as well as construction possibilities such as braiding, twisting, knitting, plaiting, wrapping, and gluing.

ROPE CONSTRUCTION

Egyptians on the Mediterranean worked with twisted and braided ropes 3,000 years ago, as did seamen 12,000 miles away in Asia. Their ropes, knots, and splices were much like those we use today, except that ropes of strong synthetic fibers have all but replaced plant fibers over the past few decades. With increased international shipping, ropes from all over the world are now evident in large commercial harbors.

Any rope is a bundle of textile fibers combined in a usable form. For example, a ½-inch-diameter (12 mm) nylon rope might have 90,000 tiny fibers, each with a tensile strength of 2 ounces (56.7 g), giving it a potential breaking strength of 11,000 pounds (4,950 kg) if the fibers could be pulled in such a way that each achieved its maximum strength. The 90,000 fibers can be bonded, twisted (laid), or braided, or these construction techniques can be combined in one rope. Regardless of the construction, the actual breaking strength of the finished rope will be less than the potential strength of its aggregate fibers due to a shearing action on the twisted fibers when the rope is loaded. This effect is most extreme in laid rope: the U.S. standard for ½-inch (12 mm) three-strand nylon rope, for example, is a breaking strength of 5,800 pounds (2,610 kg); for ½-inch nylon double-braid, it's 15 percent higher.

The old standby, three-strand twisted nylon rope, is the most economical rope available today, at about half the cost of double-braided nylon. It consists of fibers (often nylon, but sometimes polyester or polypropylene) spun into yarns, which are then formed into the strands. Nylon three-strand is commonly used for anchor rodes and mooring and docking lines—applications where its strength, pronounced stretchiness, resistance to chafe, and reasonable cost are all appreciated.

Double-braid rope came into use with the discovery that careful design and construction could induce a braided core to share a load equally with its braided cover. When you work with this rope, you must preserve the original coat-to-core spatial relationship to retain its inherent strength, so tie the Slip Knot—called

3

for in the splice directions for this construction—both properly and tightly.

Dacron double-braid is stronger than three-strand twisted nylon rope (or three-strand or single-braid Dacron, for that matter), but it is also nearly double the price for ½-inch (12 mm) rope, and the difference in cost should be considered against the line's intended use. (Dacron is a DuPont trade name for polyester, and the two terms are often used interchangeably.) Whenever the breaking strength of a rope is critical, the manufacturer's specifications should be consulted. Some low-cost rope on the market is made to look like double-braid, but it is not, so check the product carefully and deal with reputable suppliers.

Polyester double-braid rope is low-stretch and resists kinking and hockling; it handles well and is good for halyards and sheets.

Single-braid (also known as solid-braid) polyester is more supple, less expensive, stretchier, and somewhat less strong and durable than double-braid. It's useful for multipart mainsheets or vangs where ease of handling is prized and minimizing stretch matters less than it does for, say, jibsheets.

Braid with three-strand core is another common rope for running rigging on yachts. As its name implies, the outer cover is braided, in this case with 16 plaits or braids. The core, a three-strand twist, carries most of the strength. Often called Marlow, for its English manufacturer (Marlow Ropes, Ltd.), it is sold with standard and fuzzy covers, the latter being soft on the hands and holding knots well. The covers are available in colors—a convenience when, for example, one must find a halyard quickly in a maze of running rigging. Marlow can be difficult to find in some areas.

Dacron braid with a Dacron parallel-fiber core is another rope with most of the strength in the core. It stretches much less than double-braid and, pound for pound, it is as strong as stainless steel wire (see Wire Halyard Replacement Chart), so there is a trend toward using it to replace wire on recreational nonracing sailboats. In the United States, Sta-Set X (New

WIRE HALYARD REPLACEMENT CHART, IN. (MM)		
7 × 19 Stainless Wire	Braid with Parallel Core Sta-Set X	Double Braid Samson XLS 900
⅛ (3)	³⁄₁₆ (5)	⁵⁄₁₆ (7)
⁵⁄₃₂ (4)	¼ (6)	⅜ (9)
³⁄₁₆ (5)	⁵⁄₁₆ (7)	⁷⁄₁₆ (11)
⁷⁄₃₂ (6)	⁵⁄₁₆ (7)	½ (12)
¼ (6)	⅜ (9)	⁹⁄₁₆ (21)

This chart is for general comparison only. Follow the manufacturer's specific recommendations for all working loads.

England Ropes) is a popular brand. This rope is also stiff and a poor choice where bend and flex are important, such as when a line must pass through a block.

Hollow-braid rope of polypropylene floats and is most often used for water-ski towlines and around life rings.

Nylon eight-plait rope, also called square braid, is common on commercial vessels. It consists of four-strand pairs, one member of each pair having right-laid yarns and the other having left-laid yarns. (To determine the direction of the lay, consider the rope with its end pointing away from you. Right-lay spirals up and to the right.)

More rounded than eight-plait, twelve-plait rope is used most often for towing hawsers. The plaited ropes are easy to inspect for damage and can be dropped in a heap on deck without hockling.

Inexpensive rope such as clothesline, often sold precoiled in hardware stores, is not suitable for marine use.

SYNTHETIC ROPE MATERIALS

Once there were only ropes made from plant fibers such as flax, hemp, jute, sisal, cotton, and later, manila. Then there were the popular synthetics: nylon, polyester (Dacron), and polypropylene. Now, from research labs around the world, new higher-strength rope fibers with more names than can easily be remembered are available for discriminating rope users. Spectra, Dyneema, Kevlar, Danline, Cerfilene, EuroSteel, Ice-line, Certran, copolymer, Vectran, Technora, Zylon, aramid, and high-modulus polyethylene fiber—the choices can bewilder mariners, and the names are often misused and misunderstood. We will tell a few tales about some of the more popular rope fibers so that you old salts can converse with the technocrats of the rope world.

Dyneema is the trade name used in Europe by a Nether-landish company called DSM for a very high-strength, high-modulus polyethylene fiber. In the United States, this product is sold under the trademark Spectra (AlliedSignal Inc.). Another company that is using this fiber is Colligo Marine, which is sell-ing a Dynex Dux line, which it markets as Colligo Dux, which is said to be easier to splice than other fiber rigging. Until the advent of this polyethylene fiber with extremely high molecular orientation, the only rope fiber stronger than nylon was Kevlar (DuPont), an aramid fiber.

Both Kevlar and Spectra ropes, as well as many of the new rigging materials, are at least twice the strength of equal-diameter nylon rope, and they have hardly any stretch. Dyneema and products using a similar material or a portion of that mate-rial, are said to "creep" instead of stretch. Kevlar is ten times as strong as steel, pound for pound, and Spectra is six times as strong as steel. These ropes would be everywhere if they didn't cost six times as much as nylon or Dacron. Kevlar and Technora, another newly developed synthetic material, are susceptible to UV damage, so need to be encased in a braid cover. (Kevlar is not as popular these days, due to advances in other materials.)

One of the first uses of Kevlar rope was in a U.S. Navy float-ing dry dock, where it enabled line handlers using no power to maneuver ships precisely as they entered the dock. This job had previously required heavy steel wire and power winches.

Many of the largest tankers use docklines of Spectra, having found that the high initial cost is quickly recouped by savings from fewer injury claims by crewmembers and docking personnel handling the lighter lines. Large fishing trawlers have replaced their wire-rope tackles and whips with braided Spectra line. Spectra seems to last forever, while the steel-wire rope would last only a month lifting heavy nets full of fish many times a day.

Spectra and Dyneema both float in water, yet another major factor in their use as tugboat bow and stern lines. You can melt these high-tech polyethylenes with a soldering gun or an open flame. They burn in the presence of a flame but self-extinguish when the flame is removed. Spectra and Dyneema come in many colors, but white and shades of gray are most common. Strong, durable, supple, soft to the touch, low-stretch, and easier to handle than Sta-Set X, Spectra is finding increasing favor as halyards on spare-no-expense sailboats.

Right now, the most promising new rope fibers are the copolymers, which are chemical mixtures primarily of polyethylene and polypropylene. Organic chemists have teamed up with textile engineers to invent these extremely strong and durable rope fibers, and rope manufacturers around the world now have extruders turning out light, strong, low-stretch copolymer fibers that make a supple rope at a very reasonable price. Copolymer is much stronger, easier to handle, and only a little more expensive than polypropylene, and it will likely make polypropylene rope obsolete within a short time.

One of the earliest uses of copolymer was in the New England lobster-fishing industry. Lobster fishermen use a tremendous amount of rope with their traps, and it would be hard to find anyone who knows rope better than one who makes his or her living handling pot warps every day. Prior to 1950, these ropes were sisal and manila. With the advent of synthetics, polypropylene became the fiber of choice because it was cheap, it floated, and it didn't rot. Everyone on the coast of New England remembers these colorful ropes washing up on beaches everywhere, the predominant yellow becoming a symbol of the lobster industry. But recently, copolymers have almost wholly supplanted polypropylene. Copolymer fibers are so good that even poorly made rope works well. These fibers will soon be everywhere in braided and twisted ropes. Leading brands include Cerfilene, Steelline, and EuroSteel.

As if all these new rope materials and constructions weren't enough, yet another innovation is becoming increasingly popular of late: rope coatings. A coating of urethane is available in a variety of colors and can be applied over various synthetics. The coating is tough and durable, considerably reduces abrasion, and practically eliminates snagging.

SUMMARY OF ROPE CHARACTERISTICS

Both the materials and the construction of synthetic ropes mandate splicing techniques that were never needed with natural fibers. For example, manila, a natural fiber, holds its shape after it has been unlaid, but nylon changes shape very quickly as the strands slip away from each other and divide into yarns. The splicer must adapt to this tendency by sealing the strand ends as described in the rest of this book.

GENERAL CHARACTERISTICS OF SYNTHETIC MARINE ROPE MATERIALS

Material	Strength	Stretch	Shrinkage	Flotation	Cost	Common Uses
Nylon	strong	stretches	shrinks	sinks	moderate	mooring lines and docklines
Polyester (Dacron)	strong	low-stretch	low-shrink	sinks	moderate	sheets and halyards
Polypropylene	low-strength	low-stretch	low-shrink	floats	economical	water-ski towlines
Aramid	very strong	low-stretch	no-shrink	sinks	high	running rigging
High-Tenacity Copolymers	strong	low-stretch	low-shrink	floats	economical	sheets and tackles
High-Tenacity Polyethylene (Spectra and Dyneema)	very strong	low-stretch	no shrink	floats	high	running rigging

QUICK GUIDE TO STRENGTH OF ROPE MATERIALS

Diameter in Inches of Three-Strand or Double-Braid Nylon Rope

	$1/16$	$1/8$	$3/16$	$1/4$	$5/16$	$3/8$	$7/16$	$1/2$	$5/8$	$3/4$	$7/8$	1
Diameter in millimeters	1.5	3	5	6	8	9	11	12	16	19	22	25
Braid size	2	4	6	8	10	12	14	16	20	24	28	32
Circumference in inches	$3/16$	$3/8$	$5/8$	$3/4$	1	$1\,1/8$	$1\,1/4$	$1\,1/2$	2	$2\,1/4$	$2\,3/4$	3
Weight in feet per pound (kg)	400 (268	200 134	100 67	65 44	40 27	30 20	20 13.4	16 10.7	10 6.7	7 4.7	5 3.4	4 2.7)
Breaking strength in pounds (kg)	200 (90	400 180	750 337.5	1,000 450	2,000 900	3,000 1,350	4,000 1,800	6,000 2,700	10,000 4,500	17,000 7,650	20,000 9,000	25,000 11,250)

Aramid (Kevlar)—40 percent heavier than nylon; more than 200 percent stronger
Copolymers—20 percent lighter than nylon; about the same strength
Polyester—20 percent heavier than nylon; about the same strength
Polyethylene (Spectra and Dyneema)—20 percent lighter than nylon; 200 percent stronger
Polypropylene—20 percent lighter in weight than nylon; 20 percent weaker

Note: This chart is for three-strand and double braid rope of the same weight and quality. The safe working load of rope is about 10 percent of its breaking strength. In all critical situations, consult the manufacturer's local recommendations.

Rope manufacturers are combining materials to create a vast offering of ropes. For instance Samson combines Dyneema and polypro to creat its XLS Extra-T braid, a popular choice for halyards and sheets on many cruising sailboats.

SMALL STUFF

Small stuff is cordage of less than $3/16$-inch (5 mm) (to the recreational boater) or $1/2$-inch (12 mm) (to the commercial mariner) diameter. When constructed of firm, spliceable manila or nylon, it is favored by the boatowner for light-duty use and decorative projects.

Definitions within the rope industry differ, however, and some also group the following with small stuff!

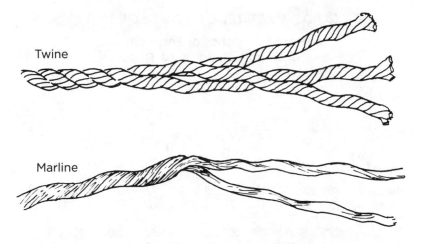

Twine

Marline

- **Twine** doesn't look like rope, although it is composed of fibers. It is usually less than ³⁄₁₆ inch (5 mm) in diameter. Waxed whipping twine is constructed of nylon or polyester and coated with wax to make whipping and seizing easier. The wax also protects against weathering.
- **Marline** consists of two strands of hemp, left-laid, and is coated with tar to protect against weathering, giving it a characteristic burned odor. It can be used for lashing or seizing.

ROPE CARE

It's foolish to buy good rope and then treat it carelessly because rope that is damaged will have a reduced breaking strength and a shorter life. Here are some ways to preserve the life span of your rope:

- To take rope off a storage reel properly, avoiding kinks, twists, or hockles in the line, let the reel rotate freely around a horizontal pipe suspended or supported at both ends.
- Store rope in a clean, dry area, off the floor, out of sunlight, and away from acid fumes.

- Keep rope from chafing against standing rigging and rough surfaces. Be wary of rusty or sharp chocks, bitts, and winches that will abrade the rope. Pulleys and blocks should be correctly sized and should turn freely.
- If a rope is chafed or frayed, cut out the damaged portion and splice. A good splice is safer than a damaged section.
- It is not generally necessary to oil or lubricate rope; if you do, use a product that is specifically designed for that purpose.
- Use whipping, tape, or an end splice on the bitter end of the rope to prevent unlaying.
- Check rope often for deterioration, opening the lay of three-strand and plaited rope for inspection.
- If rope is dragged over the ground, rocks and dirt can be picked up. Eventually, these particles can work into the rope, cutting the fibers.
- The proper way to dry a line is to lay it up on a grating in long fakes to allow good air circulation, thus preventing mildew and rot.
- Don't hesitate to wash synthetic rope by hand. Coil and tie it loosely, wash with a mild soap, then lay it out to dry.
- Don't use a rope in a situation where strength is critical if the rope has ever been subjected to a sudden, heavy load.
- A smooth taper will result in a more efficient splice.

SPLICING TOOLS

It's part of the splicing tradition to use tools that aid in separating the strands of rope. Just as high-tech rope and synthetic materials require new splicing techniques, they also mandate specialized tools to facilitate those procedures.

The Swedish fid is used for three-strand, eight-plait, and twelve-plait rope. The pointed end separates tightly twisted strands, and the concave blade allows individual strands to be

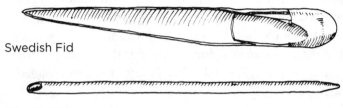

Swedish Fid

Tubular Fid

pulled into position. It is easiest to work with a fid that is in proportion to the diameter of the rope, but any fid that is not too small to guide the rope will do. Swedish fids increase in circumference with length and are available in lengths of 6 inches for about $7.20, 12 inches for $15.00, and 15 inches for $55.30 (these prices are approximates for shore areas; if you're inland, prices are probably higher).

Tubular fids aid in splicing double-braid rope, which consists of a hollow braided core surrounded by a braided cover. When the core is removed from the cover during splicing, the cover becomes a hollow tube. The tubular fid, also called a Samson fid, guides the rope through these passageways as the splice is worked.

The fid has a pointed end to ease movement through the rope and an indented end where the working end of the rope

APPROXIMATE LENGTHS OF FID SECTIONS, IN. (MM)			
Rope Diameter	Short	Long	Full
¼ (6)	2 (51)	3½ (89)	5½ (140)
⁵⁄₁₆ (8)	2½ (64)	4¼ (108)	6¾ (171)
⅜ (9)	3 (76)	4¾ (120)	7¾ (197)
⁷⁄₁₆ (11)	3½ (89)	6 (152)	9½ (241)
½ (12)	4 (101)	7 (178)	11 (279)
⁹⁄₁₆ (14)	4¼ (108)	8 (203)	12¼ (311)
⅝ (16)	4½ (114)	9½ (241)	14 (356)

is inserted. It is important that this be a snug fit, so the fids are made in sizes corresponding to standard rope diameters. If you have on hand a fid that is only slightly too large, the rope can be held in place with tape.

Measurements taken on the rope during splicing commonly use portions of the appropriate fid's length as units. A full fid length is the entire length of the fid; short and long fid lengths are marked on the fid. (See Approximate Lengths of Fid Sections table.) Tubular fids range in price from about $6.50 for the ¼-inch-diameter (6 mm) to $14 for ⅝-inch (16 mm).

A special splicing tool sold by Marlow Ropes, Ltd., manufacturer of braid with three-strand core, is necessary to splice that rope. The tool is usually available where the rope is sold and consists of a small-diameter wire with a hook at one end and an eye at the other. The hook is used as a handle; the eye, threaded with one or more of the core strands, is pulled behind.

Splicing Tool

A Uni-Fid (New England Ropes, Fall River, Massachusetts) is needed to splice braid with parallel core. This rope has a core of parallel fibers wrapped in a gauze-like material, all within a braided cover. The tool consists of a small-diameter wire with a hook smaller than that on the Marlow splicing tool. A pointed end on the Uni-Fid is pushed through the rope, while the hook, which has been inserted through the gauze, follows behind.

Uni-Fid

The Uni-Fid, like the tubular fid, is divided into fid lengths, and the table comparing fid lengths to inches applies equally to it.

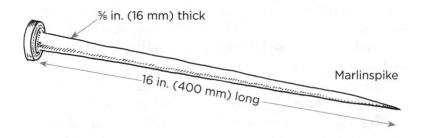

⅝ in. (16 mm) thick

16 in. (400 mm) long

Marlinspike

The venerable marlinspike shown here will easily splice wire ½ to ¾ inch in diameter. A marlinspike is usually made of steel with a tip tapered like a duck's bill. This tool comes in a variety of sizes; I've seen them from 3 inches to 5 feet (75 mm to 1.5 m). Costs range from $20 to $65, depending on size, and are available from Trawlworks.

The two needlelike tools here are helpful when splicing some of the smaller sizes of "braided" ropes. These two implements are special favorites of mine. The long, thin needle with the eye is called a *sacking needle*. It's an ideal tool for pulling rope strands into place or rope cores into, out from, or down coat centers. The other tool (I've forgotten where I found it) was the tool of choice when John Darwin and I developed the copolymer splice. Ropes are classified as textiles, so any tool or instrument associated with any kind of sewing is of possible use to the rigger, knot-tier, or splicer. For instance, a stainless steel set of forceps is a most helpful alternative to needle-nose pliers when it's necessary to dive into the center of a fancy knot or tiny splice.

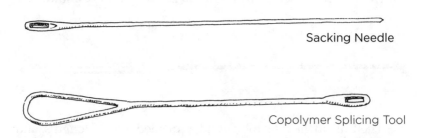

Sacking Needle

Copolymer Splicing Tool

These needles "knit" fishing nets and, like their cousin the weaver's shuttle, they hold and dispense cordage to grow the cloth. The needles come in different sizes to assist in making different-sized mesh. Also available from Trawlworks, these range in cost from just over $1 to $8.

When applying seizing, short sections of service (chafe gear), or applying service to smaller-sized ropes or wires, these needles are very helpful. They hold a lot of cordage and provide a comfortable grip while applying the twine under tension.

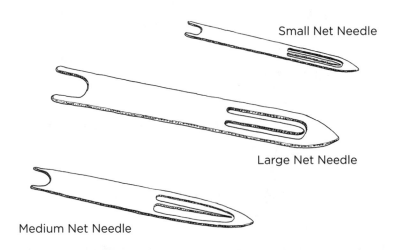

Small Net Needle

Large Net Needle

Medium Net Needle

A handmade serving tool, the *heaver* (see next page) is the arborist answer to the sailor's serving mallet. This tool is easy to master and easy to make. Any hardware store can supply the hardware. Use a band saw to shape the body and fashion the fork end. Drill the hole for the screw, then sand, stain, and varnish.

Not all splicing tools are used to manipulate rope during the working of a splice. The thimble is such a tool; it is a teardrop-shaped metal support for an Eye Splice, with a grooved outer edge for the rope.

Variations of the Eye Splice are found throughout this handbook, showing its popularity and virtuosity despite differences in rope construction and materials. Without a thimble, it is

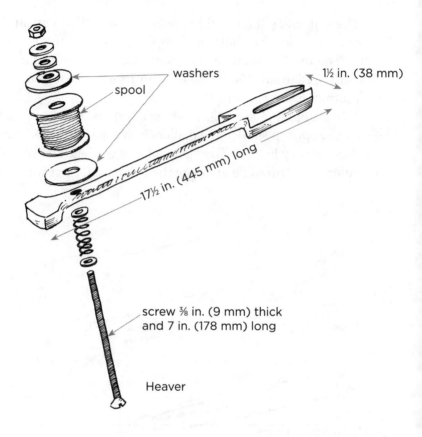

washers

1½ in. (38 mm)

spool

17½ in. (445 mm) long

screw ⅜ in. (9 mm) thick
and 7 in. (178 mm) long

Heaver

effective for light-duty use, such as on a topping lift or dinghy painter. With a thimble, the Eye Splice is ready for heavy use, when wear and chafe must be considered. A thimble should be used whenever the line will be attached to chain, swivels, or shackles, such as on the anchor end of an anchor rode.

Thimbles are available in only one eye size for any given diameter of rope. If a larger eye is needed for light-duty use and

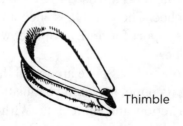

Thimble

some protection is desired, service can be placed over the crown of the eye to substitute for a thimble.

If you can't locate any of these tools locally, you can order them from me at The Marlinspike Artist, 360-C Gooseberry Road, Wakefield, Rhode Island 02879, U.S.A., 401-783-5404.

Three-Strand Twisted Rope

Technique is important to preserve splice strength, even with basic three-strand rope, which is sold in sizes ranging from ⅛ to 2 inches (3 to 50 mm) in diameter.

EYE SPLICE

*This is the most common splice.
Take care that the tucks lie neatly, and that you
complete at least three or four rounds of tucks
(the Cordage Institute recommends a minimum of
four rounds of tucks for all splices in three-strand).*

TOOLS & MATERIALS

Three-strand twisted rope
Swedish fid
Vinyl tape or whipping twine
Scissors or sharp knife
Hot knife or heat source
Ruler
Thimble (optional)

Unlay (i.e., untwist) the rope for 2 or 3 inches (50 to 80 mm) and tape each of the three individual ends or seize them tightly with twine (see chapter 13). Tape again at the point where the unlaying should end; for this splice in ¾-inch (19 mm) rope, that would be about 16 inches (400 mm) from the working end for four tucks. Add the amount of rope necessary to form the eye, or loop. Tape again. This spot is called the throat of the splice (see next page).

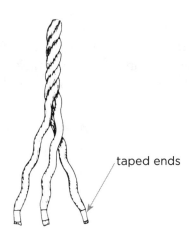

taped ends

Unlay back to the first piece of tape. To avoid a twist in the eye of the finished splice, untwist the rope just half a turn between the pieces of tape.

To do the first tuck, raise a strand just below the tape on the standing part of the rope and insert the middle working strand under it. You can usually do this with your fingers, but if the rope is twisted too tightly, use a Swedish fid (see page 12). Insert this splicing tool under the strand, and then place the middle working strand through the fid. Pull the strand into place and remove the tool.

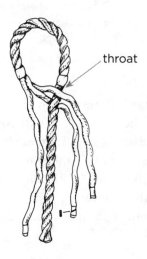

throat

The first time you work the splice, place a single hash mark on the strand that you just tucked. Numbering the working strands should help you to keep track of the tucking process.

Tuck the next working strand over the strand you just tucked

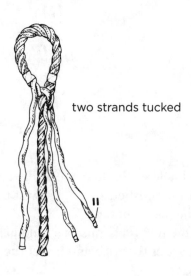

two strands tucked

under, and under the strand just below it. Mark this with two hash marks.

Turn the entire piece over. You have one working strand left to tuck, and there is one strand left in the standing part of the rope that doesn't have a working strand under it. Make this tuck, continuing to work counter to the lay, or twist, of the rope (left to right in the drawings). Mark with three hash marks.

The first round of tucks is now complete. Tighten if necessary by pulling on the strand ends.

Take care when you tuck that you use all three strands in each round, and that you tuck under a strand in the standing part of the rope and not under one of your working strands.

Make three more rounds of tucks unless the rope is nylon, which holds better with five or six rounds.

For a smooth, better-looking splice, finish with the California method: After the rounds of tucks are complete, the first strand is left as is. The next strand is tucked once (as in the beginning steps), and the last strand is tucked twice.

Cut the ends off close, seal or melt the ends of synthetic rope with a hot knife or match, and remove the tape.

DECORATIVE EYE SPLICE

The decorative knot set at the neck of this dressed-up version of the Eye Splice does not affect its strength, but you should position the knot to avoid chafing when the splice is in use.

TOOLS & MATERIALS

Three-strand twisted rope
Swedish fid
Vinyl tape or whipping twine
Scissors or sharp knife
Hot knife or heat source
Ruler

Unlay (untwist) the rope for 2 or 3 inches (50 to 80 mm), and tape each of the individual ends or seize them tightly with

twine (see chapter 13). Tape again at the point where the unlaying should end. For this splice in ¾-inch (19 mm) rope, that would be 24 inches (600 mm) from the working end of the rope. Add the amount of rope necessary to form the eye and tape again at the throat of the splice.

Unlay the rope back to the first piece of tape. To avoid a twist in the eye of the finished splice, untwist the rope just a half turn between the pieces of tape.

To do the first tuck, raise a strand just below the tape on the standing part of the rope and insert the middle working strand under it (A). You can usually do this with your fingers, but if the line is twisted too tightly, use a Swedish fid.

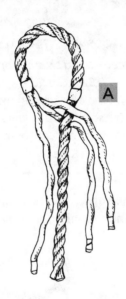

Tuck the next working strand over the strand you just tucked under, and under the strand just below it (B).

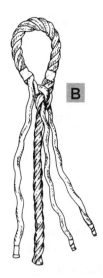

Turn the entire piece over (C). You have one working strand left to tuck, and there is one strand in the standing part of the rope that doesn't have a working strand under it. Make this tuck, continuing to work counter to the lay of the rope (left to right in the drawings).

Take care when you are tucking that you use all three strands in each round, and that you tuck under a strand in the standing part of the rope and not under one of your working strands.

The first round of tucks is now complete; tighten by pulling on the strand ends. To this point, the procedure is identical to that for the basic Eye Splice.

Now tie a Double Wall and Crown Knot as follows. Hold the throat of the splice between your thumb and forefinger with the strands emerging upward and spreading over the top of your fist, like the petals of a flower. To begin the wall knot, the first step in this three-step knot, take any strand and, moving counterclockwise, lead it over the strand next to it. (We will call this the second strand.) Allow the bight (loop) formed to remain prominent because you will need it later.

The second strand leads under the first strand, then under the third strand, as in the drawing. The third strand then leads under the second strand and up through the bight formed in the first step. This sounds complicated, but if you follow the illustration as you work, you'll see it is straightforward.

Gather the knot evenly, but keep it loose.

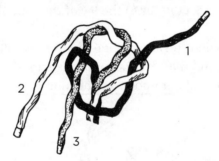

Take any strand and, continuing to work counterclockwise, lead it over the strand next to it, leaving a bight. Lead the second strand over the first strand, then over the third strand. Lead the third strand over the second strand and down through the bight.

The third and final step doubles the entire knot; this is the simplest part of the entire process. Beginning with any strand, duplicate its journey through the knot by eyeballing, poking, and wiggling it. (You left the knot loose in anticipation of this step.)

The strand's journey began near the point where its end now emerges. Guide the end back into the knot at that point and retrace the circuit—in effect, doubling the strand. Take care as you work that you don't separate other parallel pairs. It's so easy once you get rolling that you have only to stop yourself from going too far. If the strand starts to appear in triplicate, you need to back up a little. Repeat this process for all three strands, and you'll have doubled the knot. Now cinch the strands firmly and evenly.

For a smooth, better-looking splice, finish with the California method: After three full rounds of tucks (five with nylon rope), the first strand is left as is. The next strand is tucked once (as in the beginning steps), and the last strand is tucked twice.

Cut the ends off close, seal or melt the ends of synthetic rope with a hot knife or match, and remove the tape.

RING SPLICE

This splice attaches the working end of a rope to a ring or clew. Chafing between the ring and strands is minimal if the first round of tucks is pulled tight. Many sailors and fishermen use it to attach rope to chain, but directions for a safer, more professional Rope-to-Chain splice are given in chapter 11.

TOOLS & MATERIALS

Three-strand twisted rope
Swedish fid
Ring
Vinyl tape or whipping twine
Scissors or sharp knife
Hot knife or heat source
Ruler

Unlay the rope 2 or 3 inches (50 to 80 mm) and tape or seize each of the individual strands. Tape where the unlaying is to end. For ¾-inch (19 mm) rope, that would be 12 inches (300 mm) from the working end for a three-tuck splice; 16 inches (400 mm) for four tucks. Unlay the rope to the tape.

Pass the first strand on the left (Strand A) through the ring from front to back and around the ring, coming out to the right of itself. Work Strands B and C the same way, then pass Strand C to the left, over itself, and back between itself and Strand B. Draw up this round of tucks tightly and remove the tape.

To work the second round of tucks, pick up the middle

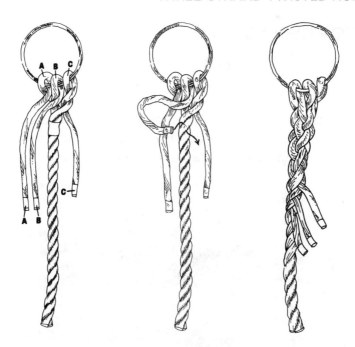

strand (B), pass it over the base of the third strand (C), and tuck it under the strand below (A).

Pick up the working end of Strand A, then pass it over Strand B and under the strand below. It will come out where Strand B tucked in on this second round. Remove the tape.

For a smooth, better-looking splice, finish with the California method: After three or four full rounds of tucks (five with nylon rope), the first strand is left as is. The next strand is tucked once and the last strand is tucked twice.

Cut the ends off close; seal or melt the ends of synthetic rope with a hot knife or match.

SHORT SPLICE

This is the strongest splice for putting two lengths of twisted rope together. The rope thickens at the splice, so it should not be used when a line must pass over an exact-sized pulley or through an opening only slightly larger than itself. In these situations, it is better to use a whole length of rope.

TOOLS & MATERIALS

Three-strand twisted rope (two pieces)
Swedish fid
Vinyl tape or whipping twine
Scissors or sharp knife
Hot knife or heat source
Ruler

Unlay one end of each rope for 2 or 3 inches (50 to 80 mm) and tape or seize the six individual ends. Continue unlaying; for ¾-inch (19 mm) rope, 16 inches (400 mm) in each rope is ample for a four-tuck splice. Tape to prevent the ropes from unlaying farther.

Interlace, or marry, the two pieces of rope so that each strand is parallel to the corresponding strand of the other piece.

To hold the splice together, place a temporary seizing of tape or twine where the two pieces join.

The first tuck of the round is started by placing one strand over the standing part of its corresponding strand and under the next. In most cases, this can be done with your fingers, but if the rope is twisted too tightly, use the Swedish fid to smooth the way.

Rotate the work and repeat until all three strands are tucked. One round of tucks is now complete; finish on the other side of the seizing in the same way.

Remove the seizing and tighten the splice by pulling on the strand ends.

Repeat all the tucks three more times. For nylon rope, continue for a total of five or six rounds.

For a smooth, better-looking splice, finish with the California method: After four full rounds of tucks, the first strand is left as is. The next strand is tucked once, and the last strand is tucked twice.

Cut the ends off close, seal or melt the ends of synthetic rope with a hot knife or match, and remove the tape.

Three-Strand Short Splice

END SPLICE

The bitter end of a rope is often finished with whipping; this splice is a good alternative when improved grip is important.

TOOLS & MATERIALS

Three-strand twisted rope
Swedish fid
Vinyl tape or whipping twine
Scissors or sharp knife
Hot knife or heat source
Ruler

Unlay about 3 inches (75 mm) of rope and tape or seize the individual ends. Tape where the unlaying should end. For this splice in ¾-inch (19 mm) rope, that would be about 16 inches (400 mm) from the working end for a four-tuck splice. Unlay the rope to the tape.

Hold the rope at the tape between your thumb and forefinger with the strands emerging upward and spreading over the top of your fist, like the petals of a flower.

To begin, crown the three strands. To do this, take any strand and, moving counterclockwise, lead it over the strand next to it (we will call this the second strand). Allow the resultant bight, or loop, to remain prominent, because you will need it later.

The second strand leads over the first strand, then over the third strand. This third strand then leads over the second strand

and down through the bight formed in your first step. The crown is now complete; draw it up tightly.

Remove the tape or seizing. For the first round of tucks, raise a strand on the standing part of the line and insert any adjacent working strand under it. You can usually do this with your fingers, but if the rope is twisted too tightly, use a Swedish fid.

Tuck a working end over the strand you just tucked under, and under the strand just below it.

Turn the entire piece over. You have one working strand left to tuck, and there is one strand left in the standing part of the rope that doesn't have a working strand under it. Make this tuck, continuing to work counter to the lay of the rope.

The first round of tucks is now complete. Tighten if necessary by pulling on the strand ends.

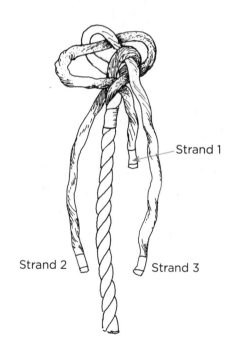

Strand 1

Strand 2

Strand 3

Repeat the series of tucks three more times, unless the rope is nylon, which holds better with five or six rounds.

For a smooth, better-looking splice, finish with the California method: After the rounds of tucks are complete, the first strand is left as is. The next strand is tucked once (as in the beginning steps), and the last strand is tucked twice.

Cut the ends off close, seal or melt the ends of synthetic rope with a hot knife or match, and remove the tape.

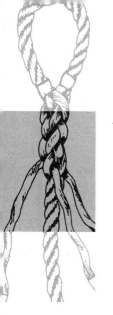

Three-Strand Splicing Projects

These splicing projects are fun as well as practical, but shop carefully for your rope so you don't work for hours and then end up with a frazzled mess. If necessary, spend a few cents more for good-quality, three-strand twisted rope or small stuff.

Use ¼-inch (6 mm) nylon or spun Dacron for the key lanyard and leash and collar; use manila or combination rope for the railing. Ask the salesperson to unlay a short portion of the rope after heat-sealing or taping the three strands and check to see that each strand holds its individual twist. If the yarns fly apart, or if the rope does not retain its shape, search for better rope. Remember to ask the salesperson to tape the rope to keep it from unlaying farther on your trip home.

KEY LANYARD

*This is a simple, attractive lanyard
to hold keys or a knife.*

TOOLS & MATERIALS
Three-strand small stuff: 26 inches (650 mm) of ⅜₆- or ¼-inch (5 to 6 mm) rope
Ring
Vinyl tape or whipping twine
Scissors or sharp knife
Ruler

A 26-inch (650 mm) piece of small stuff will give you a finished lanyard length of about 12 inches (300 mm). Attach the ring using the ring splice with at least five tucks; allow 6 inches (150 mm) for the splice. On the other end, form the loop, allowing 8 inches (200 mm) for the decorative eye splice with five tucks.

Directions for the ring splice and decorative eye splice are given in chapter 2.

DOG COLLAR AND LEASH

This is a classy but inexpensive set for your dog.

TOOLS & MATERIALS
Three-strand twisted rope
1 or 2 rings
Spring-tension clip
Vinyl tape or whipping twine
Scissors or sharp knife
Ruler

For a collar of ½-inch (12 mm) rope, allow enough to comfortably encircle the dog's neck, plus 12 inches (300 mm) for the splices.

For a loose collar, attach both ends of the collar to the same ring using ring splices. For a choke-style collar, use a ring splice to attach a ring to each end of the collar.

Allow 5½ feet (1.7 m) of rope for a 4-foot (1.2 m) leash. Attach the clip to one end using a ring splice. Finish the other end with an eye splice, making the eye large enough for your hand.

Directions for the ring splice and eye splice are given in chapter 2.

ROPE RAILINGS WITH
DOUBLE WALL AND CROWN KNOT

This is an unusually pretty way to frame a favorite area in the garden or to line a walkway. It can also be used as an inexpensive safety railing around docks and piers. The double wall and crown knot serves as a stop-knot where the rope passes through a post.

TOOLS & MATERIALS
Three-strand twisted rope
Vinyl tape or whipping twine
Scissors or sharp knife
Ruler

For directions on tying the double wall and crown knot, see the decorative eye splice in chapter 2.

CLIFF'S SAILING HARNESS

My friend Cliff gave me the pattern for this smart harness, which is easy and inexpensive to make. The harness is light and takes up very little room when not in use. Dacron works best for this; nylon tends to shrink and harden with age and wetting.

TOOLS & MATERIALS
25 feet (7.6 m) of ⅜-inch (9 mm) three-strand Dacron rope
1 heavy-duty snaphook
Tape
Sharp knife or scissors
Whipping twine and needle

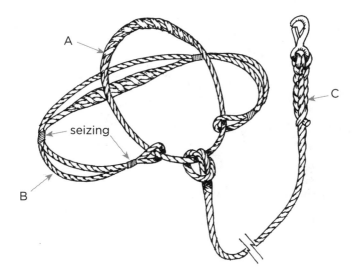

The harness consists of three pieces: an endless loop that fits over the head (A), another endless loop that, when doubled, goes around your trunk (B), and a tether with snaphook (C).

To make A, cut off a length of rope 40 inches (1.02 m) long. On both ends, measure back from the end 4 inches (100 mm) and tape at that spot. Unlay both ends back to the tape, taking care to preserve the three strands. Execute a short splice, as

39

described in chapter 2. Three rounds of tucks on each side are adequate for this purpose.

To make B, you will need to get your chest measurements, over foul-weather gear if need be. Double the measurements; to that amount, add 10 inches (250 mm). Cut the second piece of rope equal to that measurement. Execute another short splice in this piece, but only after wrapping each end around endless loop A. Secure piece B with four seizings, as visible in the drawing on the previous page.

The rope that remains is for the tether, which should be long enough to let you move around but short enough to keep you in or within reach of the boat. Ten feet (3 m) or thereabouts is a common compromise. At one end, splice in a 4-inch (100 mm) eye; at the other end, splice in a 9-inch (225 mm) eye. The splices on this piece should have five rounds of tucks.

Double-Braid Rope

Double-braid is the most common and widely used configuration of ropes made from polyester, aramid, and polyethylene (Spectra). Double-braid rope is composed of a braided core inside a braided coat, or outer covering. Sometimes various materials are blended to optimize such qualities as strength, weight, stretch, and cost. For example, rope with a Spectra-aramid core and polyester coat is as strong as 7 × 19 wire of half the diameter, stretches about the same, and weighs less. But no matter the materials used, both core and coat contribute to the strength of the rope. It is important, therefore, that when your splice is finished, the coat covers the core smoothly and evenly, as it did when manufactured. To accomplish this, be sure to tie a Slip Knot, as directed for each splice, to keep the core from sliding up inside the cover while you work.

The weak spot on spliced rope lies on the standing side of the splice, where the rope is first disturbed. Tapered ends are usually buried there, so follow the tapering directions carefully.

EYE SPLICE

*Follow these steps to put an eye or a thimble
at the end of double-braid rope.*

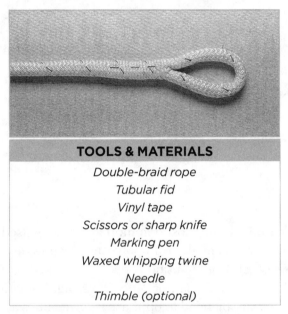

TOOLS & MATERIALS
Double-braid rope
Tubular fid
Vinyl tape
Scissors or sharp knife
Marking pen
Waxed whipping twine
Needle
Thimble (optional)

Trim the end of the rope evenly, cutting off melted ends, or tape the end to be spliced. Using a tubular fid (see page 12), measure one full fid length from the tape and label this point with an R. (To determine the appropriate fid for the rope you are using, see page 12.)

Add the amount of rope necessary to form the eye or the loop around the thimble (see page 16), if one is used. Mark an X there, at the throat of the splice. This is a complicated splice to complete with a thimble, so measurements are critical.

Move up the rope at least five full fid lengths and tie a tight slip knot. Return to the X and gently push aside the strands of the coat (the rope's outer covering) to expose its inner core. Pull a small loop of the core through the coat as carefully as possible, and draw a single hash mark across the core. Then continue pulling out the core until its working end is completely exposed, and tape the end. Work the cover down into place to confirm that the X and hash mark are aligned and equal distances from the coat and core end, respectively.

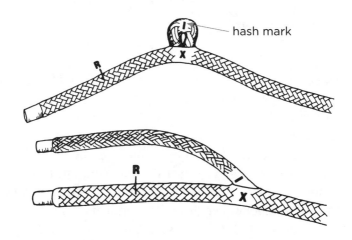

Now pull out more core, this time from the standing part of the rope, and measure one short fid length from the single hash mark. (Short and long fid lengths are marked on tubular fids; for the measurement in inches, see page 12.) Make two hash marks there (see drawing next page).

Continue along the core for one full fid length plus one short fid length, pulling out more from the standing part if necessary. Make three hash marks.

For maximum strength in the splice, you will need to draw the rope's outer coat into its core and then its core into the coat. It will help to remember that the coat is marked with letters and the core with hash marks.

Pinch the taped end of the coat and insert it into the hollow end of the fid, taping it in place. Push the fid into the core at two hash marks and out at three hash marks. Be careful not to twist the coat. Pull until the R comes into view. The core will bunch up as you do so, but this will correct itself later.

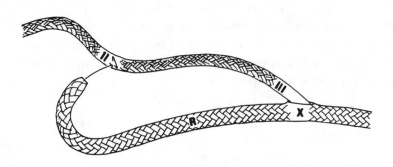

To taper the end of the coat, work toward the fid from R, and count off seven sets of picks, or parallel ribs, that run clockwise; mark this spot with a T. Continue toward the fid, marking every seventh pair with a dot so you will know where to cut.

Now go back to the R, this time marking the counterclockwise picks for tapering. To offset the tapering on these picks, mark your first dot at the fourth pair. From there, mark every seventh counterclockwise pair until you reach the fid.

Remove the fid and the tape. Cut and remove a single strand at each marked pick along the coat.

While holding the core, pull the coat until the T shows beyond the two hash marks. Take care not to lose the end of the tapered coat into the core.

For extra strength, the core end should be drawn through the coat, past the throat of the splice, and into the standing part of the rope. Measure from the X toward the slip knot one short half of the tubular fid; label this spot with a Z.

Tape the pinched end of the core into the hollow fid end. Insert it into the coat at the T and work it through the coat as far as you can without a struggle. Depending on the size of the eye, the fid may not reach the necessary exit point in one pass. If this happens, bring the fid out of the coat, pulling some of the core with it. Then simply reinsert the fid into the same hole and work it farther through the coat. Continue this snaking process until the fid exits at the Z. Be sure not to snag any strands of coat with the fid at reentry points.

Draw up the slack until the coat-to-core unions formed at the T and two hash marks meet at the top of the eye. Now that this portion of the splice is complete, you should hide the end of the coat by smoothing the coat from the T to the three hash marks. Take your time and be thorough so the tapered end slides completely into the core at the three hash marks.

Remove the fid and smooth the pucker. Poke through the coat at the X to make some visible mark on the core inside. Also mark the core where it exits from the Z. Pull on the core tail until the mark you made under the X exits from the coat at the Z. Unbraid the tail, comb and fan it; then cut it off at a 45-degree angle between the two marks. Hold the rope gently at the union, and ease the coat from there around the eye until the core tail disappears. Trim the ends.

Take a firm grip of the rope close to the slip knot or attach it with a hook to a firm surface. If you measured carefully from the beginning of the splice, there should be enough slack in the bunched coat to roll down off the tail end and the coat-to-core joints.

Bunching may occur at the throat as the doubled core section and displaced yarns are distributed. If it does, roll and flex the rope or gently tug on the tail of the core. Begin this process gently but firmly. As you proceed, you may have to exert more pressure, perhaps to the point of pounding on the throat with a wooden mallet.

Double-braid splices—like most splices—are easy to take apart because they are designed to be pulled on, not pushed. To hold this splice firm, lock-stitch it in the following way.

Pass a needle threaded with twine all the way through the throat, leaving a tail of about 8 inches (200 mm). Make three complete stitches running along the standing part of the rope. Remove the needle from the twine and thread it with the tail end. Sew three stitches parallel to the first, but 90 degrees around the rope's circumference from them. Bring the two ends together through the standing part of the rope and tie with a square knot, shown in chapter 27.

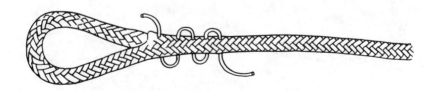

Turn the rope 90 degrees and repeat the stitches. Trim the twine ends.

If you wish to protect the eye with a leather chafing strip, you'll need to apply this before you put in the lock-stitching (see chapter 13).

In the 1960s, Samson Cordage Works, now Samson Rope Technologies (Ferndale, WA), developed a superior rope double braid. The quality of the product is excellent, and the price is reasonable.

END-TO-END SPLICE

*Here is a way to make an endless loop
or to join pieces of double-braid rope.*

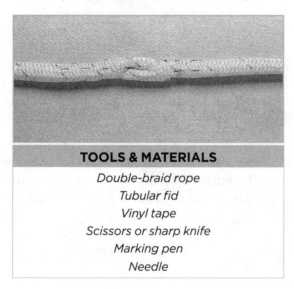

TOOLS & MATERIALS
Double-braid rope
Tubular fid
Vinyl tape
Scissors or sharp knife
Marking pen
Needle

To make an endless loop in double-braid rope, you should allow four full fid lengths of rope to accommodate the splice. (See page 12 for the relationship between rope diameter and fid size.) Do not use double-braid for an endless loop smaller than 2½ feet (750 mm) in circumference; for those splices, use three-strand twisted, eight-plait, or twelve-plait rope.

For maximum strength of an end-to-end splice, it is essential that the smooth, one-to-one relationship between coat and core be restored as completely as possible. This can be difficult, but pounding on the rope with a wooden mallet will loosen the strands and ease the job.

On each piece, draw the coat down over the working end of the core, removing as much slack as possible from the coat. Cut each end so that the coat and core are the same length, and tape to prevent unlaying.

Measure six full tubular fid lengths from each end and tie a slip knot.

Measure one full fid length from each end and label these reference points with an R. (Short and long fid lengths are marked on tubular fids; for the measurements in inches, see page 12.)

Mark an X one short fid length up the standing part of each rope from the R.

At the X, gently push aside the strands of the coat to expose its inner core. Pull out a small loop of core through the coat as carefully as possible, and draw a single hash mark across the top of the core.

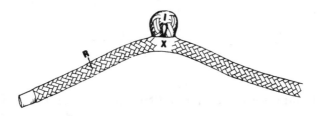

Pull out the working-end core completely at the X and tape its end. Smooth the coat and core to confirm that the X and hash mark are aligned at equal distances from the end. Now pull out more core—this time from the standing part of the rope—and measure one short fid length from the single hash mark. Draw two hash marks there (see page 50).

Continue along the core, pulling out more from the standing part if necessary, and mark three hash marks at a distance

totaling one full fid length plus one short fid length from the two-hash-mark point.

Repeat with the second rope.

To taper the coats, work with each separately. From the R, toward the working end, count off seven sets of picks, or parallel ribs, that run clockwise and mark this spot with a T. Continue to work toward the end, placing a dot at every other clockwise pick until five have been marked, so you will know where to cut.

Beginning again at the T, mark every other counterclockwise pick.

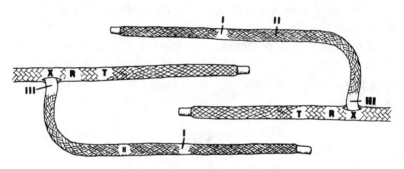

Cut and remove the marked strands between the T and the working end. Untape the end while pulling the strand loose. Repeat with the second rope.

Pinch the taped end of either coat and insert it into the hollow end of the fid; tape it in place. Push the fid into the core of the other rope at two hash marks and out at three hash marks, being careful not to twist the coat. While holding the core, pull until the T is aligned with the two hash marks. Some bunching of the core will occur, but this will resolve itself later.

Repeat this procedure with the second rope.

Each core must now be reinserted into the coat that runs

through its center. Tape the pinched end of either core into the hollow fid end and insert the fid at the T. Work it through the coat and exit at the X. Repeat with the other rope.

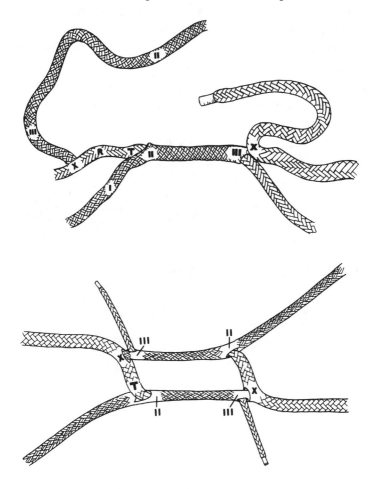

Draw up the slack by pulling on both core and coat tails until the coat-to-core crossovers are snug.

Hold the rope at a joint and smooth all the puckered braid, working in both directions away from the joint. Take your time and be thorough so the tapered end of the coat slides completely into the core at three hash marks. Remove the fid from the core tail. Repeat with the second joint.

Cut off the core tails flush at the coat.

51

Take a firm grip of the rope close to a slip knot. If you measured carefully from the beginning of the splice, there should be enough slack in the coat to pull down over one of the coat-to-core joints and the tail ends. Repeat to cover the second joint with slack from the opposite direction.

Bunching may occur as all the extra yarns running through the coat are distributed. If it does, roll and flex the rope. Begin this process gently but firmly, gradually applying more pressure as necessary. You may have to pound the rope with a wooden mallet.

An opening through the splice is normal, but it should not be any longer than the diameter of the rope.

Lock-stitch with needle and thread (see page 46).

END SPLICE

*This is a neat alternative to whipping
a double-braid rope.*

TOOLS & MATERIALS

Double-braid rope
Tubular fid
Vinyl tape or whipping twine
Scissors or sharp knife
Marking pen

If the end of the rope has been heat-sealed, cut it off and tape it to keep it from unlaying. Measure one full fid length from the working end of the rope and mark this spot with an X.

Move up the rope at least five full fid lengths and tie a tight slip knot.

Return to the X and gently push aside the strands of the coat to expose its inner core. Pull out a small loop of core through the coat as carefully as possible, and make a single hash mark across the top of the core. Pull out the core completely and tape its end. Confirm that the X and hash mark are aligned at equal distances from the end.

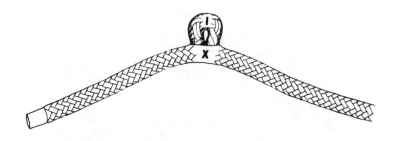

Now pull out more core, this time from the standing part of the rope, and measure one short fid length from the single hash mark. (Short and long fid lengths are marked on tubular fids; for the measurement in inches, see page 12.) Make two hash marks there.

Continue along the core, pulling out more from the standing part of the rope if necessary, and make three hash marks at a distance totaling one full fid length plus one short fid length from the two hash marks.

Now draw the rope's outer coat into its core. Remember that the coat is marked with letters, the core with hash marks. Pinch the taped end of the coat and insert it into the hollow end of the fid; tape it in place. Push the fid into the core at two hash marks and out at three. Be careful not to twist the coat. Pull until the splice is snug but not buckled.

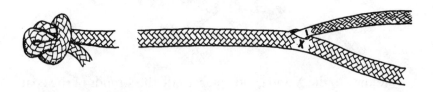

Remove the fid and tape. To taper the coat tail, unbraid and fan it, then mark one-third of a full fid length up the coat. Cut at an angle from the opposite bottom corner.

Smooth the core, working from two to three hash marks; if you measured carefully, the coat tail will slip into the core.

Starting from the slip knot, work the coat down over the core, pulling an ever-deepening fold into the coat ahead of your fingers. When you reach the end, the fold you have created should be deep enough to envelope the entire splice. The crease of the fold where it terminates at the working end of the splice will appear like the half-inverted finger of a rubber glove when you slip it off your hand.

Cut the core off flush with the coat. Smooth it again to ensure that any exposed core is completely covered.

ROPE-TO-WIRE SPLICE

A Rope-to-Wire Splice is often used to attach rigging wire to a halyard. With double-braid rope, both the core and coat must be spliced into the wire.

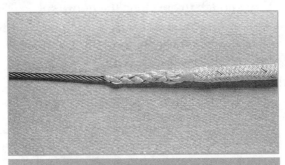

TOOLS & MATERIALS

Double-braid rope
7 × 19 stainless steel wire
Swedish fid
Wire cutters
Vinyl tape
Scissors or sharp knife
Hot knife or flame source
Ruler
Waxed whipping twine
Marking pen
Homemade splicing jig (optional)

The 7 × 19 stainless steel wire consists of six strands (bundles), each containing 19 yarns, and a central core (see page 140). The wire should be suitable for rigging and should measure about one-half the rope's diameter.

For this splice, the wire must be tapered to a core plus one strand. Cut one strand at 6 inches (150 mm) from the end, one at 5 inches (125 mm), one at 4 inches (100 mm), and two at 3 inches (75 mm). Tape around the wire at each level.

Tie a slip knot 8 feet (2.4 m) up the braided rope to keep the coat from creeping up the core more than necessary. If the end of the rope has been heat-sealed, cut it off; push the coat 4 feet (1.2 m) up the core. Cut off 6 inches (150 mm) of the exposed core and tape the end.

Measure up the core 21 inches (530 mm) and mark.

Insert the tip of the tapered wire into the hollow core 8 inches (200 mm) from the working end, and gently and carefully work it up through the core until it reaches the mark at 21 inches (530 mm). (See art next page.)

Tape lightly around the core and wire at the 21- and 8-inch (530 and 200 mm) locations to hold your work snug. (From this point on, the work will go more smoothly with a jig, which I'll describe in the next section.)

Working carefully, unbraid the core to the 8-inch (200 mm) mark and divide the yarns into three groups. You will get a much neater splice if you tape neighboring yarns together.

To splice the first group of yarns into the wire, slip the fid under two wire strands in the direction opposite the twist of the wire (see drawing, page 58). Lay the rope along the groove from the handle to the tip; pull the rope into place and remove the tool. Repeat with the other two yarn groups, carrying on around the back of the wire to make a complete wrap with each group. Continue until three rounds of tucks are completed. Remove one-third of each group and tuck the fourth round; remove another third and tuck the fifth round. Cut the ends very close.

Melt any ends into the wire by passing a lighted match close to the cut ends. Use some care here or you could melt your whole splice.

Beginning at the slip knot, milk the coat by squeezing it while sliding your hand gradually toward the wire. Work in short, overlapping sections and do not pull on the coat. When you have removed all slack, the core-to-wire portion of the splice should be completely covered. Whip over the coat where the splice on the core ends. (Instructions for whipping are given in chapter 13.)

For the coat-to-wire portion of the splice, unbraid the coat, smooth the yarns out straight, and—as you did previously with the core—divide the yarns into three groups. These groups must also be spliced into the wire, but they will be inserted so they travel in the same direction as the wire strands. Insert each group under the appropriate wire-strand pair, completing one round of tucks.

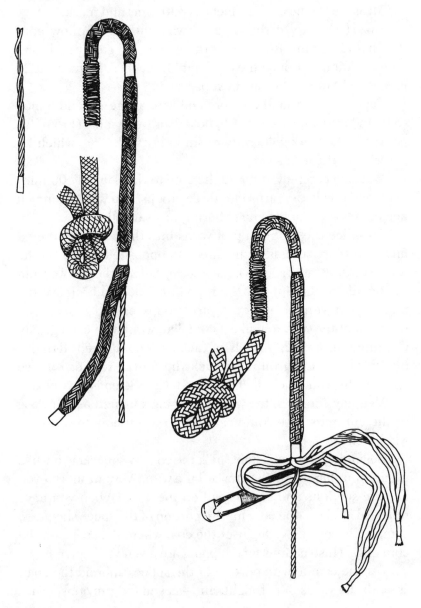

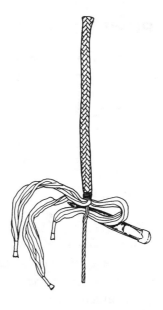

To taper this splice, repeat the tucks, omitting a portion of each yarn group at each tuck, until only a few yarns remain. Cut the ends close to the wire and carefully melt the yarn ends with a match.

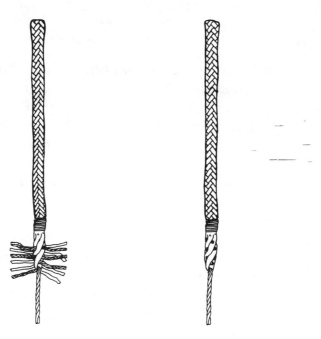

JIG FOR THE ROPE-TO-WIRE SPLICE

A jig supplies me with an extra pair of hands that never gets tired when I'm doing rope-to-wire splicing.

TOOLS & MATERIALS

1 length of 1 × 5½ × 24-inch wood (for base) (25 × 140 × 610 mm)
2 pieces of common 2 × 8s
(actual dimensions 1⅝ × 7½ inches/
41 × 190 mm), 5½ inches (140 mm) long
2 hinges
2 Perko #769 clamp stays
(available at any good marine store)
6 wood screws, #8 × 2½ inches (64 mm)
Screws for hinges and clamp stays
2 bolts (cap screws) ⁵⁄₁₆ × 2½ inches
(8 × 64 mm)
¼ inch (6 mm) square head bolt
1 pair of 6-inch (150 mm) pointed-nose
vise grips
1 pair of 6-inch (150 mm) regular vise grips
2 pieces of ½-inch (12 mm) copper tubing,
¾ inch (19 mm) long

Start by drilling a ½-inch (12 mm) hole through each 2 × 8, centered at midlength (2¾ inches/70 mm from either end) and approximately 1½ inches (38 mm) down from the top edge. Along the lower semicircular arc, 2 inches (50 mm) from the center of each ½-inch hole, drill about five ⁵⁄₁₆-inch (8 mm) holes.

Next, saw off the tops of the two 2 × 8s and save. The cuts should be 1½ inches (38 mm) down from the top edges, through the centers of the ½-inch (12 mm) holes.

Install the saved tops, using the hinges and the clamp stays.

Now screw the two 2 × 8s upright to the 24-inch (610 mm) piece of wood using the #8 × 2½-inch (64 mm) screws. On my jig, I installed one of the 2 × 8s 1 inch (25 mm) from one end, and the other 6 inches (150 mm) from the other end, but these dimensions are a matter of preference. Leaving some space at the ends will allow you to clamp the jig to a work surface.

Once the jig is together, you will realize that you no longer have two true ½-inch (12 mm) holes where the wire and rope go through, because the board was cut directly at the holes. It will be beneficial if you run your ½-inch drill through them again while they are clamped shut.

To keep splinters at bay and to help your rope from becoming snagged, sand the entire jig and round the edges and corners slightly.

Pound the two pieces of copper tubing over the jaws of the 6-inch (150 mm) regular vise grips, one piece on each jaw. This will help prevent damage to the wire.

Wrap the jaws of the pointed-nose vise grips with electrician's tape to help prevent damage to the rope.

Set your piece into the jig, positioning the rope-to-wire marriage at the center. Clamp the copper-clad vise grips onto the wire on the outside of the upright, flat against the wood. If your wire is of small diameter, you might notice that it floats around in the hole. I cure this by taping in a "bushing" of leather or cardboard. Next, clamp the pointed-nose grips onto the rope, again, outside the upright and flat against the wood. Insert a bolt into

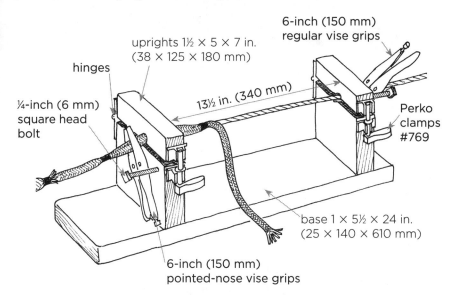

6-inch (150 mm)
regular vise grips

uprights 1½ × 5 × 7 in.
(38 × 125 × 180 mm)

hinges

¼-inch (6 mm)
square head
bolt

13½ in. (340 mm)

Perko
clamps
#769

base 1 × 5½ × 24 in.
(25 × 140 × 610 mm)

6-inch (150 mm)
pointed-nose vise grips

one of the $\frac{5}{16}$-inch (8 mm) holes so the vise grips cannot spin around. You'll know on what side to set it in just a moment.

Our next job is to ease some twist out of the wire. Rotate the copper-clad vise grips so that the lay of the wire loosens. Note: if the pointed vise grips on the rope rotate along with the copper-clad vise grips, the wire won't unlay, so set the bolt as described. The wire will start dipping and curving; some wires do this more than others. I have found that some wires need two full rotations while others need only a half turn. When you think you have a little of the twist removed, stop the copper-clad grips with a bolt. Take care here because if the grips slip out of your hand, it will whirl around, knocking your knuckles with some force. You will be able to tuck only once or twice before having to adjust the grips again.

CORE-TO-CORE EYE SPLICE

Use this alternative eye splice on double-braid rope such as Spectra for which—according to the manufacturers' specifications— the primary strength lies in the core.

TOOLS & MATERIALS

Double-braid rope
Tubular fid
Vinyl tape
Scissors or sharp knife
Marking pen
Waxed whipping twine
Needle
Thimble (optional)

Place a fresh piece of tape on the rope end where the eye is to be spliced to keep the rope from unlaying. Using a tubular fid, measure two full fid lengths from the tape and label this reference point with an R.

Add the amount of rope necessary to form the eye, or for the loop around the thimble, if one is used. Mark an X here, at the throat of the splice. (This is a complicated splice to complete with a thimble, so measurements are critical.)

Move up the rope at least eight full fid lengths and tie a tight Slip Knot.

Return to the X and gently push aside the strands of the coat to expose its inner core. Pull out a small loop of core through the coat as carefully as possible. Draw a single hash mark across the top of the core.

Pull out the working-end core completely, and tape its end.

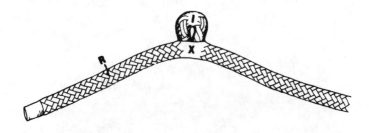

Now pull out more core, this time from the standing part of the rope, and measure one short fid length from the single hash mark. Make two hash marks there.

Continue along the core three full fid lengths plus one short fid length, pulling out more core if necessary. Make three hash marks.

Pinch the taped end of the core and insert it into the hollow end of the fid; tape it in place. Push the fid into the coat at the R and out at the X. You should now have the core exiting twice at the X. Pull the core through until the single hash mark lines up with the R, then hold it firmly in position while you smooth the coat from the R to the X. Mark the tail core where it exits at the X with a band around the core.

Insert the fid (with the core end still taped to it) into the core at the two hash marks, run it through the core, and pull it out at the three hash marks—in effect, pulling the core through itself. Pull until the band lines up with the two hash marks.

To taper the tail that exits at the three hash marks, fan it. Then measure from its working end one-third of a full fid length, making a mark at that point. Cut at an angle from the opposite bottom corner to the place marked.

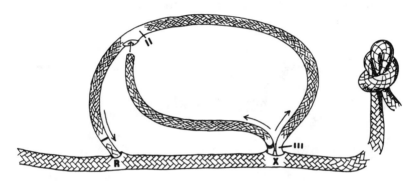

The distance between I and II is one short fid length. The distance between II and III is three full fid lengths plus one short fid length.

Hold the rope where the band on the core and the two hash marks meet, and smooth the core toward the loose tail. The tail should slip into the core if your measurements were correct.

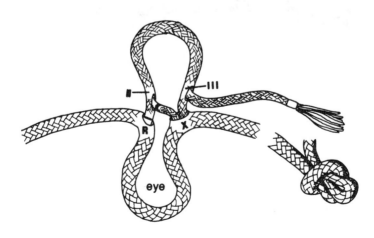

Core disappears into coat at X.

Attach the slip knot to a sturdy hook, or have an assistant hold it. Smooth the coat from the knot toward the splice until the whole core is enveloped by the coat, taking special care around the eye. Detach the slip knot from the hook, and attach the eye there instead.

Pull tightly both the standing part of the rope and the coat tail (from the R to the working end) toward you.

Apply a tight layer of tape around the throat for a distance equal to one short fid length.

Apply a tight whipping over the tape (see chapter 13).

Cut the tail close.

REDUCED VOLUME END-TO-END SPLICE

Kim Houghton, owner of Rig-Rite, Inc., introduced me to this splice. Some sailboat roller-furler mechanisms require an endless loop of line for operation, and sometimes the endless-loop splice built using the manufacturer's recommended method is too bulky to reeve through the furler drum. The splice shown here has a 50 percent smaller cross section than the standard splice. Its strength is also reduced by 50 percent, but it remains strong enough for the purpose.

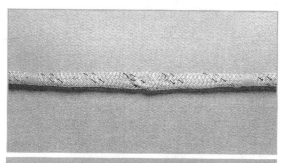

TOOLS & MATERIALS

Double-braid rope
Tubular fid to suit your rope
Tape
Marking pen
Sharp knife or scissors
Whipping twine and needle

Before executing this splice, reeve the line around the drum and through all the relevant hardware. Assuming you're leading the line back to the cockpit, you'll need the length of the endless loop to be twice the distance from drum to cockpit, plus the extra needed for the drum, the cockpit belay, and any intervening directional changes.

If the rope ends have been heat-sealed, cut off the sealed ends, then tape them to keep them from unlaying. Lay the ends out and mark the rope at two places toward each end: Mark A should be one full fid length from the ends; Mark B should be half a full fid length from Mark A.

Put a good, tight, permanent whipping right behind each of the two B marks. Now, just in front of the two B marks, separate the coat strands to expose the core. Pry them out completely and cut off the core tails flush at the coat.

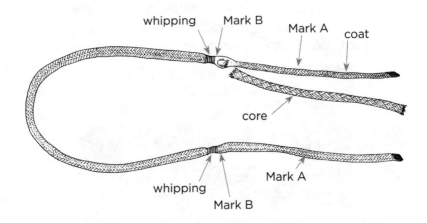

Using the fid, marry the two taped ends by interlacing one into the other at the midpoint A marks. The taped ends exit the coat at the B marks. Thoroughly milk out all the slack.

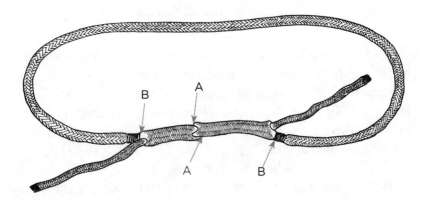

Cut the ends close, and sew the crossover at Mark B.

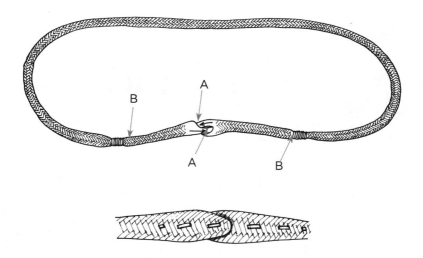

Solid-Braid Splice

This interesting splice proves that it's possible to put an eye at the end of any rope, no matter the construction.

Until World War II, rope always consisted of combed plant fibers that were twisted by stages into three strands, which in turn were twisted into a single length of rope. But then rope manufacturers found that braiding rather than twisting the strands created a smoother rope that was less prone to chafe and wear. The first such ropes were window-sash cords, from which came all sorts of single-braid cordage (also known as solid-braid because it is of uniform cross-sectional construction, without a core or hollow center).

Single-braid was soon supplanted for most purposes by today's incomparable double-braid ropes, in which an equally tensioned cover and core offer great strength and ease of splicing. We still see nylon or polyester single-braid in use for clotheslines and other light-duty tasks, however.

I learned the solid-braid splice by way of a bet. Shortly after the first edition of this book was published, Ron Denise from South Carolina visited my shop. His specialty is providing ropes, slings, and harnesses for arborists. He stayed a week, opening my eyes to a whole different world of rigging. One day, with a wicked gleam in his eye, he said, "I can splice any rope you give me." I dug around and found a length of hard-used ¼-inch (6 mm) clothesline and handed it to him, saying, "We all know it's impossible to splice hard-used rope, and this small-diameter single-braid should make it even more interesting. Good luck!" Then I watched while he set in a solid-braid splice. Ron called it a helical splice—I suppose because the weave twists around and down the rope barber-pole fashion.

I've since seen these splices used to set in the eyes of the puller ropes used by utility companies, and in lengths of rubber-coated ropes used in some places in fishing nets and gear. On pleasure boats, I've seen this splice set in flag halyards.

If the rope you're splicing is to be used under severe conditions, such as high loads or rough handling, contact the rope manufacturer for its latest splicing instructions and recommendations.

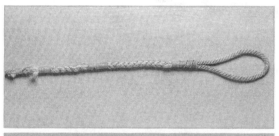

TOOLS & MATERIALS

Braided rope (flag halyard)
Scissors or sharp knife
Whipping twine and needle
Waterproof flexible adhesive
(such as that made by 3M)
Marking pen (fine)

The method of measuring is different from other splices. Instead of fid lengths, we will be using rope diameters.

Lay out your rope, forming an eye of the desired size and leaving a tail of the necessary length. To determine the length of strands necessary for the splice, measure the diameter of the rope. Allow a length of 22 rope diameters for the tail and make a mark. Remove the tape or cut off the melted end of the rope. Unlay the rope up to the mark. Don't be surprised if the unlaid portion seems unusually long: for this splice it is necessary. Again form the eye and apply a very tight seizing at the throat, measuring three rope diameters. In the illustration, the top half of the seizing is a French Hitching. To make the French hitching, which stays in place nicely especially when working with small cordage, simply tuck the end under each turn of the seizing to make a series of half hitches, with each hitch seated upon the previous one. When you snug the hitches, they should describe a smooth spiral around the rope.

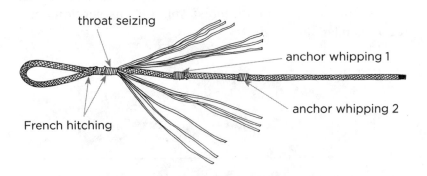

throat seizing

anchor whipping 1

anchor whipping 2

French hitching

On the standing part of the rope, put a whipping six rope diameters down from the throat and a second whipping six rope diameters down from the beginning of the first. We'll call these anchor whippings, because their function is to provide grip points along the slick standing part.

Pick up the strands at the throat and divide them into four groups.

Apply a light coating of adhesive on the standing part of the rope (where you'll be making the splice), taking care to avoid spraying the strands. Essentially, you'll be "braiding" the silky, slippery strands down around the standing part; the adhesive coating (think of it as hair spray!), while not necessary, will make the job easier. Along with the anchor whippings, it will help keep the splice in place while you tie it.

Choose one of the strand groups and wrap it down the standing part of the rope in barber-pole fashion. Fasten the end temporarily with a Constrictor Knot (see inset illustration) below the second whipping. Choose another group and wrap it down the rope in the opposite direction from the first group. Fasten that group with a constrictor knot adjacent to the first constrictor.

Wrap the third and fourth groups of strands in the same fashion, and anchor them temporarily with additional constrictor knots.

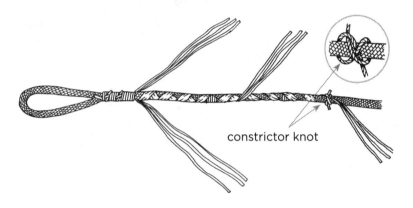

constrictor knot

Over the four groups, place a tight "cover" whipping just as close as possible down from the first anchor whipping on the standing part of the rope. Similarly, butt another cover whipping against the lower edge of the second anchor whipping. Untie the constrictor knots, and reduce the volume of the four strand-group ends by half.

Pick up the reduced strands and wrap them barber-pole fashion as mentioned previously. Fasten the ends a short distance down from the second whipping, first with a temporary constrictor knot and then a whipping. Cut and remove half the remaining strands from each group. Now you have a tapered splice, and you can end it here by trimming all the strand ends close to the last whipping. Alternatively, if you want an even gentler taper, you can halve the volume of the remaining strand groups yet again, and repeat the last step. Then trim the remaining ends close.

If you like, coat the piece with a light coating of clear spray lacquer or acrylic. After all, a four-strand, plaited, Single-Braid Splice is a true example of marlinspike art.

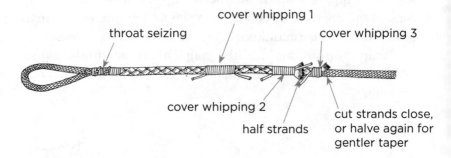

cover whipping 1

throat seizing

cover whipping 3

cover whipping 2

half strands

cut strands close, or halve again for gentler taper

SIX

Braid with Three-Strand Core

B raided rope with three-strand core can also be called 16-plait with three-strand core because the outer coat consists of 16 strands. I like Marlowbraid's fuzzy coat; it provides a good grip and, at the same time, feels good in my hands. Technically a two-part rope, it is unlike double-braid because 90 percent of its strength is in its twisted core.

This is a difficult rope to splice, but the results are worth the extra effort. Don't attempt to splice any rope of this type under ¼ inch (6 mm) in diameter, because the Marlow splicing tool (see page 13) won't fit; for smaller rope, use the solid braid splice described in chapter 5.

EYE SPLICE

TOOLS & MATERIALS
Braid with three-strand core
Marlow splicing tool
Scissors or sharp knife
Vinyl tape
Marking pen
Ruler
Whipping twine
Thimble (optional)
Swedish fid

Tie a slip knot about 5 feet (1.5 m) from the end of the rope to prevent the coat from creeping up the core more than necessary. If the end of the rope has been heat-sealed, cut it off and tape the new end to prevent unlaying.

Mark the coat 9 inches (230 mm) from the end to make room in the working end for the splice. Form the rope into an eye and mark the coat again. (Allow an extra ½ inch/12 mm if you are using a thimble.)

Push aside the threads of the coat at your second mark until the hole is large enough to expose the core. Extract the core by hooking it with a Swedish fid. Cut 3 inches (75 mm) off the core's end.

Form the eye to the proper size, this time on the core, and cut off one of the core's three twisted strands at the throat of the splice.

Move toward the working end an inch (25 mm) or so, and remove half the thickness of another strand; tape. Continue tapering and taping until the end of the core is small enough to go through the eye of the splicing tool.

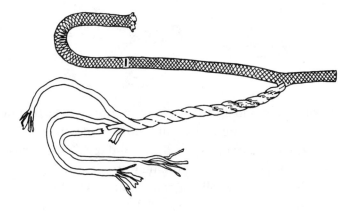

To ease the coat away from the core and make the splice easier to complete, draw out additional core from the standing part of the rope. Extract about 3 inches (75 mm) for ⁵/₁₆- and ³/₈-inch (8 and 9 mm) rope, and 4 inches (100 mm) for ⁷/₁₆- and ½-inch (11 and 12 mm) rope.

Begin at the slip knot to reposition the coat by milking it firmly while sliding your hand toward the spot where the coat and core separate. This action loosens the core and coat, and makes them easier to work with. Work in short, overlapping sections and do not pull on the coat.

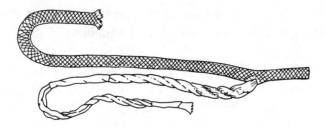

Insert the eye of the Marlow splicing tool (see page 13) into the coat where it opens for the core. Push it through the coat to exit at the throat.

Thread the core through the eye of the splicing tool and draw it back through the coat to exit with the tool at the coat opening.

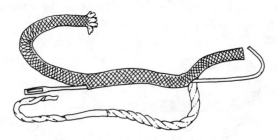

You will now gradually work all of the core ends farther down the standing part of the rope. Untape the ends, unlay the tail, comb out the strands with your fingers, and divide the yarns into three groups. Tape the ends of the new groupings.

Insert the eye of the splicing tool 12 inches (300 mm) below the mark for the throat and exit at the original coat opening. Thread one-third of the tail, located there, into the eye. Pull it through the coat and draw it out.

Repeat with the remaining two sections of core tail, bringing one out 10 inches (250 mm) and the other out 8 inches (200 mm) below the throat, pulling each time. Remove the tape from all three sections.

Pull until the union is firm and the throat closes.

Taper the coat by removing one strand at 3 inches (75 mm) from the end, two strands at 2 inches (50 mm), and four strands at 1 inch (25 mm).

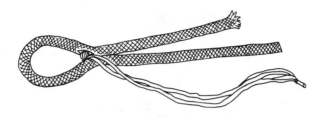

Now the working end of the coat must be pulled through the standing part of the rope. To make it easier to do this, begin a pathway by inserting the empty tool at the throat and pushing it out about 3 inches (75 mm) up the standing part of the rope; wiggle it.

Reverse the tool, entering the rope about 3 inches (75 mm) below the throat and exiting at the throat. Lace the eye with some of the shortest pieces of coat tail and pull them through. Repeat at various points around the circumference, below the throat. Pull the longer tail pieces through farther from the throat.

If you are using a thimble, insert it now. To take the slack out of the splice, hook the eye over a strong hook or knob, hold the core and cover tails, and pull firmly until the coat and core are snug.

Cut off the tails close to their exit points and firmly smooth the entire coat over the core from the slip knot to the throat. The clipped ends should slip into the rope.

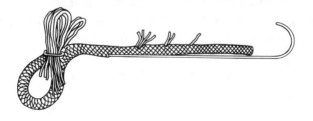

Lock-stitch with needle and thread (see page 46).

ROPE-TO-WIRE SPLICE

This is a good splice to attach rigging wire to a halyard.

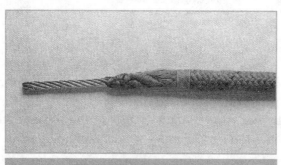

TOOLS & MATERIALS

Braid with three-strand core
7 × 19 stainless steel wire
Swedish fid
Wire cutters
Vinyl tape
Scissors or sharp knife
Hot knife or flame source
Waxed whipping twine
Marking pen
Ruler
Homemade splicing jig (optional)

The 7 × 19 stainless steel wire consists of six strands, each containing 19 yarns, and a central core (see page 140). The wire should be suitable for rigging and should measure about one-half the rope's diameter.

For this splice, the wire must be tapered to a core plus one strand. Cut one strand at 6 inches (150 mm) from the end, one at 5 inches (125 mm), one at 4 inches (100 mm), and two at 3 inches (75 mm). Tape around the wire at each level.

Tie a slip knot 8 feet (2.4 m) up the braided rope to keep the coat from creeping up the core more than necessary. If the end of the rope has been heat-sealed, cut it off; push the coat 4 feet (1.2 m) up the core, cut off 6 inches (150 mm) of the exposed core, and tape the end.

Measure 21 inches (530 mm) up the core and tape.

At that point, open the lay and set the tip of tapered wire into the rope's twisted core at a 45-degree angle. Spiral the wire into the lay of the core, continuing to within 6 inches (150 mm) of the working end. Tape into position. Unlay the core strands from here to the working end. (From this point on, the work is easier with a jig to serve as an extra pair of hands. See the jig illustration and instructions under the double-braid rope-to-wire splice in chapter 4 if you'd like to try that route.)

To splice the first rope strand into the wire, slip the fid under two wire strands in the direction *opposite* the twist of the wire. Lay the rope strand along the groove from the handle to the tip; pull the rope into place and remove the tool. For a more finished appearance, untwist the core strand as it passes under the wires.

Repeat with the other two core strands, continuing in a direction opposite the lay of the wires. Each core strand tucks under a different pair of wire strands, just as in a three-strand rope splice. Continue until five rounds of tucks are completed; cut the ends very close.

Beginning at the slip knot, milk the coat by squeezing it while sliding your hand gradually toward the wire. Work in short, overlapping sections, and do not pull on the coat. When you have removed all slack, the core-to-wire portion of the splice should be completely covered. Whip over the coat where the splice on the core ends (instructions for whipping are given in chapter 13).

For the coat-to-wire portion of this splice, untwist the coat back to the whipping. Divide the yarns into three groups, trying to keep neighboring yarns together. These yarns must also be spliced into the wire, but they will be inserted so they twist in the same direction as the wire.

To taper the end, repeat the tucks, omitting one yarn at each tuck until only seven or eight yarns remain in each group.

Cut the ends close to the wire.

Braid with Parallel Core

Parallel fibers wrapped in a gauze-like material form the core of this braid. When low stretch and high strength are critical, such as in a halyard, this rope is a good choice; if flexibility is important, double-braid is better.

EYE SPLICE

The basic directions for this splice provide a soft eye that conforms easily to small blocks. A variation, as noted in the following text, produces a hard, unyielding eye that is excellent for situations calling for a larger loop. These directions are for Sta-Set X, manufactured by New England Ropes, Inc., of Fall River, Massachusetts, the major distributor of this rope to the marine market; other braid with parallel core requires a different splice. A special splicing tool, the Uni-Fid (see page 13), is necessary to complete this splice because of the rope's parallel-strand core. Chandleries that stock this rope usually sell the fid also.

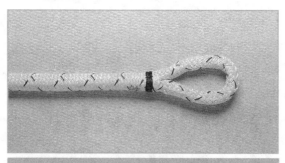

TOOLS & MATERIALS

Braid with parallel core
Uni-Fid
Scissors or sharp knife
Masking tape
Waxed whipping twine
Marking pen

Place a fresh piece of tape on the rope end where the eye is to be spliced to keep the rope from unlaying.

Tie a slip knot 12 full fid lengths from the working end to retain the one-to-one relationship between the core and coat.

Wrap a layer of tape around the rope one full fid length from the working end. (Fid sections are marked on the shipping tube for the tool.) Label this reference point with an R.

Add the amount of rope necessary to form the eye, and mark this spot with an X.

Continuing toward the slip knot, measure 1½ full fid lengths. (Note that one-half of a full fid length is *not* the same as a short fid length.) Mark this point with a Y.

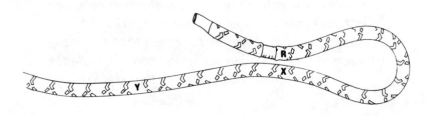

Return to the X and gently pull aside the strands of the coat to expose its inner core. Pull out a small loop using the Uni-Fid. Draw a single hash mark across the top of the core.

Pull out the working-end core completely, taper the end by cutting it at an angle, and tape. This will ease snaking of the core through the coat in a succeeding step.

Now pull out more core, this time from the standing part of the rope, and measure one short fid length from the hash mark. Place two hash marks there.

For a *soft* eye: Place a layer of tape on the standing side of this spot so it just touches the double hash mark.

For a *hard* eye: Measure from the two hash marks toward the working end of the core, the distance between the R and the X (rope set aside for the eye). Place a layer of tape on the standing side of this spot.

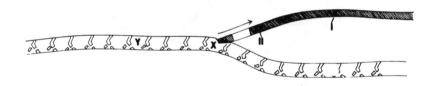

Sink the hook of the Uni-Fid into the wrapped core 1½ inches (38 mm) from the tapered end. To prevent snagging, apply a smooth layer of tape to hold the fid in place on the core.

Insert the free end of the fid into the coat at the R and work it past the X, then out through the coat at the Y. Use two hands, massaging the rope ahead of the fid. If you snag the core, back up to free it, and then proceed.

Remove the fid.

Unwind the gauze wrapping from around the parallel fibers of the tail between the tape placed for the eye and the working end. Cut it off, taking care not to cut any of the core fibers. Measure one short fid length from the working end and mark. Fan the tail and make an angled cut from the mark to the end to give a full taper to the core.

To taper the coat tail, begin at the R and count down five picks, or ridges, and mark. Continuing toward the working end, count off 15 picks and mark again. Cut the tail off square there. Unlay the coat back to the mark at the fifth pick, and make an angled cut from the fifth to the fifteenth pick.

Align the R and the two hash marks, causing the core strands to begin creeping into the coat. (Bunching usually prevents the strands from disappearing, but if they totally slip into the coat at this step, that's okay.)

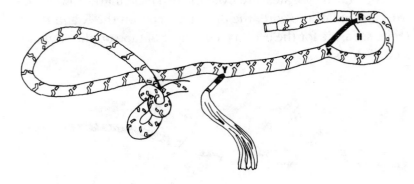

Tightly tape the tapered coat tail with masking tape; use as little tape as possible, but be sure to get all the loose ends. Smooth the coat from the slip knot down toward the eye; the core should slide back into the coat.

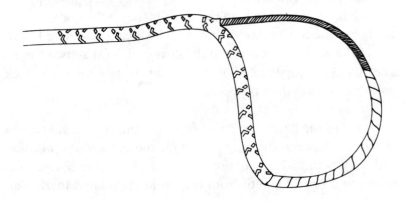

Attach the slip knot to a mounted hook, or have an assistant hold it. Smooth the coat over the core and coat-to-core joint. Begin gently, but if bunching occurs at the throat, roll and flex the area. If the coat does not move into position, use more muscle power and less finesse. You may have to pound on the rope with a wooden mallet to redistribute the strands.

Lock-stitch the splice into place (see page 46).

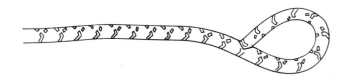

EIGHT

Hollow Braid

Splices in hollow braid work on the same principle as the Chinese finger puzzle. After the working end is passed through the braid of the standing part and into the hollow of the rope, and the fid (see below) is removed, the strands of the braid return to their factory form. In doing so, they constrict, gripping the length of the rope tightly.

A special splicing tool, or fid, is made for this rope, but these fids are hard to find, so I recommend an alternative—a knitting needle with its end cap removed, or even a length of wire coat hanger. Either can be taped tightly to the rope while you work.

EYE SPLICE

TOOLS & MATERIALS

Hollow-braid rope
Splicing tool (see chapter introduction)
Scissors or sharp knife
Marking pen

No exact measurements are needed to splice this rope, but for an eye or a loop 3 inches (75 mm) or smaller, use the Locked Eye Splice described later in this chapter.

Lay out your rope and form the necessary loop. For splicing ropes of ¼ to ½ inch (6 to 12 mm) (the most commonly used sizes), allow about 1½ to 2 feet (450 to 600 mm) for the tail.

Taper the end of the rope by cutting it at a 45-degree angle. Pinch this tapered end into the hollow of the fid or slide it like a sleeve over the knitting needle or piece of coat hanger, then tape it tightly.

Insert the splicing tool through the braid at the throat of the splice. Ease the tip of the tool down through the hollow of the rope for a distance of 8 or 9 inches (200 to 230 mm), then poke it back out through the braid. Draw the tool completely out, pulling the tail through to adjust the eye to the desired size. Smooth the rope.

Pick up the tailpiece with the splicing tool attached and mark it where it exits the braid. Then pull on the tail until an additional 3 inches (75 mm) is showing, in effect shrinking the eye. Doubling the tailpiece back on itself, insert the tool at the mark on the tail and run it back down the tail hollow 2½ to 3 inches (63 to 75 mm) before pushing it back out through the braid.

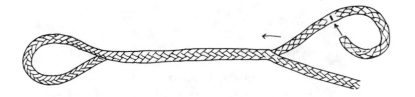

Pull the end through until the loop you have just formed in the tail disappears.

Cut the end close to the braid and push the cut strand ends back into the tail and out of sight.

Smooth the coat back into place.

Finally, work the tail back into the standing part so that the eye grows back into its proper size. As you go, note the unique property that causes this splice to hold: If you grasp the eye in one hand and hold the standing part of the rope in the other, the weave of the braid around the spliced section will tighten when you try to pull the tail back into the core, and the tail will refuse to budge. If you grasp the eye in one hand while pinching the braid opening in the throat of the splice with your other thumb and forefinger, you can easily pull the tail back through the braid until just its knobby end remains visible. Anyone who has ever played with a Chinese finger puzzle will understand why this works as it does.

LOCKED EYE SPLICE

This is an easy and quick splice to execute. It is a good method to use if the eye is 3 inches (75 mm) or smaller.

TOOLS & MATERIALS

Hollow-braid rope
Splicing tool (see chapter introduction)
Scissors or sharp knife

Lay out your rope and form the necessary eye. For rope of ¼ to ½ inch (6 to 12 mm) in diameter, allow about 10 inches (250 mm) for the tail. Taper the end of the rope by cutting the tip off at a 45-degree angle.

Push the tapered end into the hollow of the fid or affix it tightly to the splicing tool, as described for the previous splice.

Wrap the working end of the rope around the standing part to make a Half Hitch as shown in the drawing, and adjust the hitch until the eye is the desired size.

Insert the tip of the splicing tool into the standing part of the rope just above the hitch and ease the tool approximately 8 inches (200 mm) up through the standing part's core before poking back out through the braid. Pull the tool completely out and draw out the tail until snug.

Smooth the rope and cut the tail off close, tucking the cut strand ends back into the braid of the standing part until hidden from view.

END-TO-END SPLICE

*Use this splice to join two ends of
hollow-braid rope or to form an endless loop.*

TOOLS & MATERIALS
Hollow-braid rope
Splicing tool (see chapter introduction)
Scissors or sharp knife

Lay out the two ends of rope or, if you are making an endless loop, adjust to the correct size. For rope of ¼ to ½ inch (6 to 12 mm) in diameter, allow about 10 inches (250 mm) for each tail.

Taper both ends by cutting the tips off at a 45-degree angle.

Push one tapered end into the hollow of the fid or affix it tightly to the splicing tool, as described for the eye splice at the beginning of this chapter.

Measure 10 inches (250 mm) from the other working end and insert the splicing tool at this point, easing it up to the hollow core of the standing part for 10 inches (250 mm).

Bring the tool back out through the braid, trim the end close, and tuck the strand ends back into the braid and out of sight.

Repeat for the other tail, inserting the splicing tool as shown in the drawing.

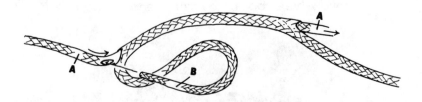

The splice will hold in use and is similar to the Chinese finger puzzle principle described for the eye splice in this chapter.

Copolymer End-to-End Splice

B ecause copolymer rope is still somewhat new to the market, its uses are still specialized. But this mix of polyethylene and polypropylene fibers is destined for increasing popularity. Copolymer is strong, easy to handle, economical, and resistant to stretching and shrinking, and it floats. Already it's replacing polypropylene as the rope of choice for New England's lobstermen.

The Copolymer End-to-End Splice is useful for attaching two lengths together without a lumpy knot. (And because of the construction of the rope [i.e., the core's two bundles of parallel strands contain the rope's strength, not the braided coat], we can't use a standard hollow-braid splice.)

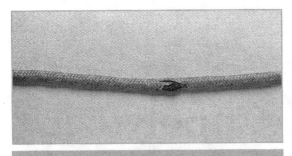

TOOLS & MATERIALS
Rope
Splicing tool (there are no specialized tools
for this rope, but the copolymer splicing
tool described in chapter 1 works well)
Scissors or sharp knife
Marking pen
Whipping twine and needle

Cut off the heat-sealed melted ends on the two ropes if necessary.

Measure back from both ends 14 inches (355 mm) and make a mark on both ropes at that spot. At your mark, separate the strands of the coat and then pry out the cores completely, back to the ends.

Now, moving farther up the two standing parts, away from the cut ends, make a second set of marks on the coats, another 14 inches (355 mm) beyond the first set.

Turn and adjust the two ends of the ropes so they face each other.

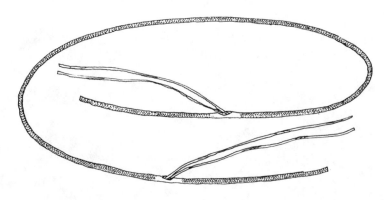

Insert the splicing tool into one of the ropes at the second mark (i.e., 28 inches/710 mm from the end). Run the tool down the center of the rope and poke just the tip out where the core exits the rope, at the first mark. Thread about 1½ inches (38 mm) of the end of the other rope's cover into the tip of the tool, then drag it back through and out at the second mark.

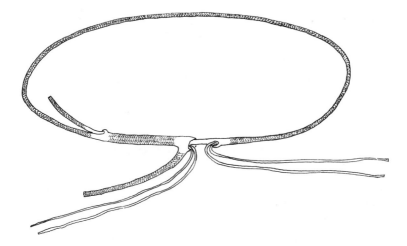

Turn the ropes and do the same to the other end.

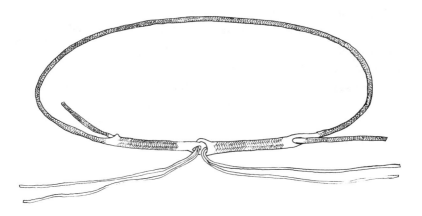

To splice in the two parallel cores, repeat what you did with the rope's covers.

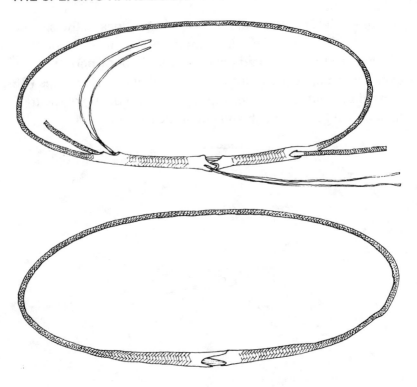

Milk out all the slack and bury the ends as shown, cutting and removing any core or cover tails.

Apply a tight whipping over the joint.

Due to the nature of this splice, some of the core will show at the marriage. You might wonder whether this splice has any real strength but, in fact, it does, due to the Chinese finger-puzzle effect described in chapter 8. Remember, too, that so far this splice has been used only with light-duty fishing gear, where it seems to work well. As this rope gains increasing acceptance, stronger, more sophisticated splicing techniques will evolve.

Eight-Plait Rope

This rope is laid with eight strands that are worked in pairs for splice strength and appearance. Available in nylon, polyester, and Spectra, this is an inexpensive construction that resists twisting and hockling and, therefore, finds favor for commercial uses. I see a lot of eight-plait line on tugboats. Because the picks have a larger surface area for abrasion, however, it doesn't wear as well as double-braid.

If the manufacturer has not color-differentiated the two right-laid pairs from the two left-laid pairs, mark either pair with a pen to simplify the splicing process. (Directions are given with each splice for the length of rope to mark.)

EYE SPLICE

TOOLS & MATERIALS

Eight-plait rope
Swedish fid
Vinyl tape
Scissors or sharp knife
Hot knife or heat source
Marking pen
Waxed whipping twine

Estimate the amount of rope you will need for the eye and mark either both right-laid strand pairs or both left-laid strand pairs for about twice this distance. Starting from the working end, count up the standing part of the rope 10 picks and seize the rope at that point with tape or twine.

Unlay the rope to the seizing, allowing the twist in the individual strands to remain. Tape the strand pairs together at their working ends (A).

Form the eye and take a painted pair of strands and tuck them at the throat under a handy unpainted pair in the standing part (B). A Swedish fid can make the process easier.

Turn the splice over and slip the other painted pair under the second unpainted pair (C). Always work so that you are tucking against the lay of the strands in the standing part. That is, if the standing pair twists from upper right to lower left, tuck under it from left to right.

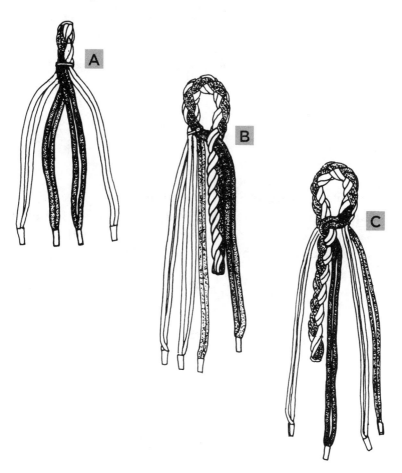

Turn your work a third time and tuck an unpainted strand pair under a painted pair. Turn again (D), and then tuck the second unpainted pair under the second painted pair. One round of tucks is now finished.

Complete *at least* two more rounds of tucks.

Cut off one strand from each pair 1 or 2 inches (25 to 50 mm) from the end. Tape or heat-seal the ends. Tuck the remaining single strands twice more, then cut and tape.

END-TO-END SPLICE

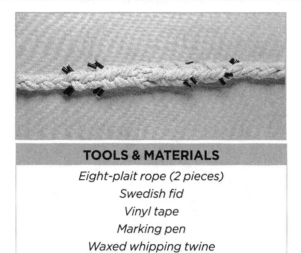

TOOLS & MATERIALS
Eight-plait rope (2 pieces)
Swedish fid
Vinyl tape
Marking pen
Waxed whipping twine

Seize each rope tightly at the ninth or tenth pick. Mark both right-laid strand pairs or both left-laid strand pairs from the bitter end of each rope to about the sixteenth pick. Remove the tape or heat-sealed tips at the working ends, and unlay the strand pairs, leaving the twist in each strand. Tape the strand pairs at their ends, taking care that they do not become twisted together.

Align the ropes end to end. To marry the ropes, lace a painted pair of strands from the right-hand rope through the corresponding painted pair on the other rope, as shown in the illustration.

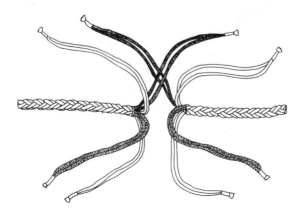

Lace the adjacent unpainted pair on the right-hand rope through the corresponding pair on the other rope.

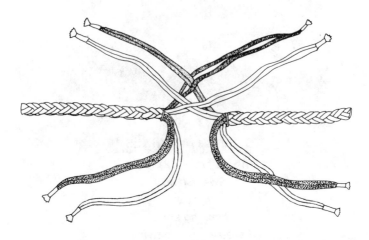

The other two strand pairs are laced in the opposite way: the painted pair on the left-hand rope is laced through the corresponding painted pair on the right-hand rope and, finally, the left-hand unpainted pair is laced through the last, opposite strand pair.

Draw the two rope ends together and seize with twine at the center to hold the developing splice in place. Remove the original seizings.

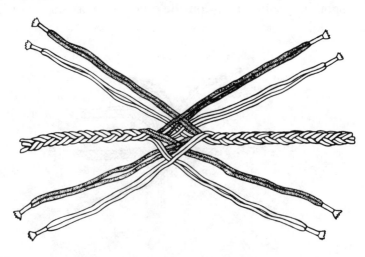

To begin the first round of tucks, insert one painted pair under the adjacent unpainted pair on the standing part of the mated rope and cinch tightly, then insert a pair of unpainted strands under the neighboring painted pair. Next, tuck the remaining painted pair and the remaining unpainted pair in the same manner, completing one round of tucks. Continue with additional tucks until 1½ inches (38 mm) of strands remain, and then repeat the procedure for the other side.

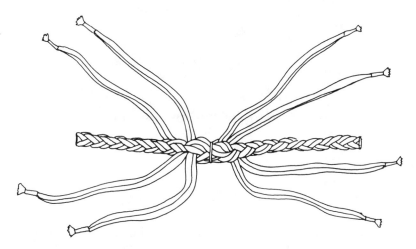

Cut off one strand from each pair. Tape or heat-seal the ends. Tuck the remaining single strands twice more, then cut and tape.

TEMPORARY EYE SPLICE

This Temporary Eye Splice is dependable and quick to execute. To be on the safe side, replace it with a standard eye splice at an early opportunity.

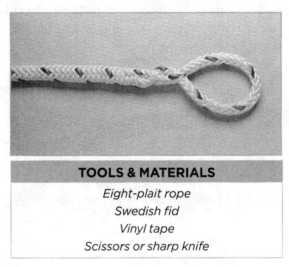

TOOLS & MATERIALS
Eight-plait rope
Swedish fid
Vinyl tape
Scissors or sharp knife

Measure off 12 inches (300 mm) for the splice and, beginning there, form the eye. At the throat, with the point of the fid, separate the strands into clockwise and counterclockwise groups.

Reeve, or insert, the tail end through the opening by the fid.

Move down three picks along the standing part from where the tail emerges, separate the strands in the same way as before, and reeve the tail back through in the opposite direction. Repeat this process twice.

Tape the tail to the standing part. The tail should be at least 3 inches (75 mm) long to allow for slippage.

Eight-Plait Rope-to-Chain Splice

Technically, this splice belongs in chapter 10 on eight-plait rope, but it deserves a chapter of its own. This splice is superior to other systems for anchor rodes because there is no knobby shackle-and-thimble connection to drag across the deck. Also, it eliminates a shackle in a position where the pin often is lost from chafe or rust.

Chain is used on an anchor rode more for its weight than its strength. It lies on the bottom and helps to convert the force pulling on the anchor from vertical to horizontal so the anchor will be less likely to break out of the bottom and more likely to hold. Chain is also more resistant to chafing on rocks and coral heads. Match your chain to the anchor and shackle, as recommended by your supplier, and choose rope of sufficient diameter to be handled comfortably and to match the breaking strength of the chain. Be careful, however, not to buy rope so big that the strand pairs can't be laced through the chain links. Make sure the rope is nylon, which is elastic enough to function as a shock absorber when the boat bucks and tugs at its anchor.

ROPE-TO-CHAIN SPLICE

The Rope-to-Chain Splice and the construction of the eight-plait rope work very well together for anchor rodes, permitting the passage of rope and chain through a bow chock or hawsepipe. The eight-plait rope is excellent: Kinks and hockles fall right out, so it need not be coiled belowdecks. If eight-plait rope is not available, twelve-plait can be used instead; no shackle is needed. Be sure to work this splice up tight; excess slack in the spliced strands could cause abrasion.

TOOLS & MATERIALS

Eight-plait rope
Chain
Sharp knife or scissors
Electrical friction tape
Serving mallet or reel-type serving tool
Whipping twine
Liquid rope seal (optional)

Measure the length of 12 links of chain to determine the required splice length for the rope. As an example, this distance is about 12 inches (300 mm) for ³⁄₁₆-inch (5 mm) chain. Pick up the eight-plait rope and measure the appropriate distance from the working end. Apply a good tight whipping (see chapter 13) at that point and unlay the rope back to the whipping. Notice the construction of the rope—four pairs of strands, each pair consisting of one strand of yarns twisted clockwise and one with yarns twisted counterclockwise.

Lay out the rope as shown.

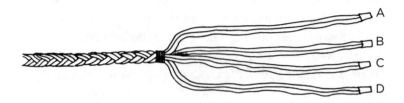

Set the first link of chain directly on top of Strand Pair A and lace these two strands up through the link. Lace Strand Pair B down through the link, making sure it crosses Strand Pair A.

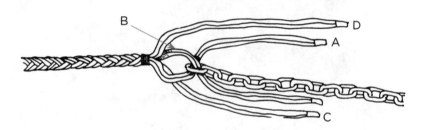

Repeat this procedure with Strand Pairs C and D through the second link, then return to Strand Pairs A and B for the third link, and so on. In this fashion, leapfrog down the chain. Two strand pairs cross through each link, and each pair skips a link before entering another from the side on which it exited in the previous pass.

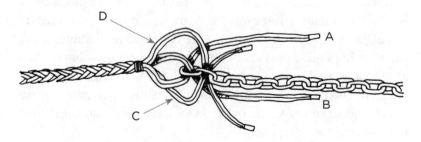

Continue this two-part process until ten links have been filled, then finish the splice on the eleventh and twelfth links. To finish, remove the tape from the strand pair ends. Separate the two strands of each pair, pass one through a link (either the eleventh or the twelfth, as appropriate) and the other around the side of the same link. Then seize the two strands together closely, as shown, to prevent movement of the rope over the chain. Seal the strands by melting them with a match or hot knife. Applying a coat of liquid rope sealer would be a plus. As a final touch, serve the entire splice tightly with small stuff (see chapter 14) to further ensure that the strands do not chafe.

Twelve-Plait Rope

Constructed of nylon or polyester, this rope is used primarily on commercial boats for hawsers, docklines, and towlines. There is no need to coil twelve-plait; you can drop it in a heap and then just give it one or two good shakes to rid it of hockles and kinks.

EYE SPLICE

This splice can be completed with your fingers, but a fid will do a neater job.

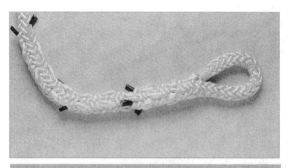

TOOLS & MATERIALS
Twelve-plait rope
Swedish fid (optional)
Vinyl tape
Scissors or sharp knife

The amount of rope necessary for this splice equals the circumference of the rope times seven (e.g., 1-inch/25 mm rope has a circumference of 3.14 inches/80 mm, so to make this splice in 1-inch/25 mm rope would require 22 inches/560 mm of rope). Determine this distance from the working end and tape the rope there. Unlay enough rope to be able to tape each of the 12 strand ends. Then unlay the rope to the tape, taking care to retain the individual twists.

Form the eye above the tape and mark the throat (see (A) next page).

Group the strands into six pairs, each pair having one strand with its yarns twisting clockwise and an adjacent strand twisting counterclockwise. Tape the pairs together (B).

Divide the six strands into two groups, taking the three strand pairs on one side (to the left of drawing (C) on next page) and reeving them directly through the middle of the rope at the mark on the throat. It is important to maintain the twist on the strands as they pass through the rope, and they must lay just

115

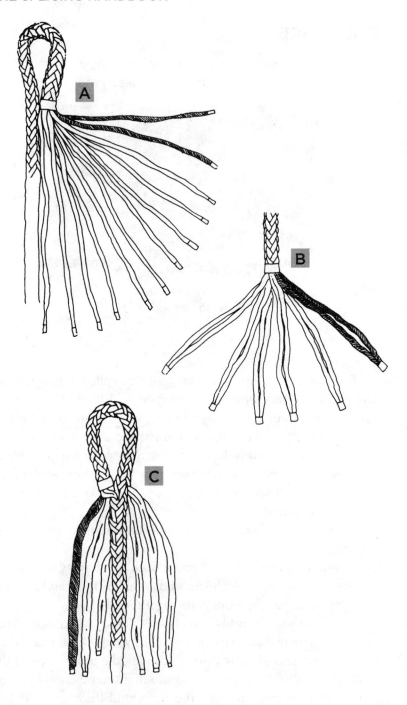

right—not too loose or too tight. Snug the strands to remove excess slack.

Begin with a convenient strand pair and tuck it under a nearby strand pair in the standing part of the rope.

Repeat with the five remaining pairs, making each tuck parallel with the one adjacent.

Complete two more rounds of tucks with each strand passing over one pair in the standing part before tucking under the next pair. Then begin tapering by trimming every other strand pair about 1½ inches (38 mm) from the standing part of the rope.

Complete another three rounds of tucks with the remaining strand pairs; then taper again, this time by cutting one strand from each pair. Retape the ends.

After another three rounds of tucks, draw up the three single strands tightly. Cut and tape their ends, leaving tails about 1½ inches (38 mm) long.

END-TO-END SPLICE

TOOLS & MATERIALS

Twelve-plait rope
Swedish fid
Vinyl tape
Scissors or sharp knife

As in the twelve-plait eye splice, the amount of rope necessary for this splice equals the circumference of the rope times seven (for each rope see next page). Determine this figure, and tape both ropes at that distance from the working ends. Unlay enough rope to be able to tape the 12 strand ends on each rope to prevent the yarns from raveling. Then unlay the ropes to the tape, taking care to retain the individual twist.

Group the strands into six pairs for each rope, each pair having one strand with yarns that twist clockwise and an adjacent strand with yarns that twist counterclockwise. Tape the ends of each pair of strands together.

To join, or marry, the two ropes, begin with any strand pair on one rope and lace it through the corresponding pair on the second. Lace the neighboring pair on the second rope through the corresponding pair on the first. Proceed in this way until all the strands are laced. Gently snug the two pieces together by drawing up the strands (see art on following page).

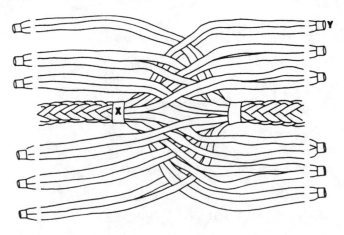

Distance from X to Y equals 7 times the rope circumference.

To make the first round of tucks, pass any convenient strand pair over one nearby strand pair in the standing part of the other rope and draw it under the next two strands. Make parallel tucks with each subsequent strand pair to complete the first round.

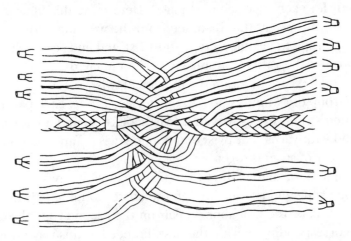

Repeat with the second rope. Then complete two more rounds of tucks, working in the same way.

To begin tapering, trim off every other strand pair about 1½ inches (38 mm) from the standing part of the rope and tape the ends.

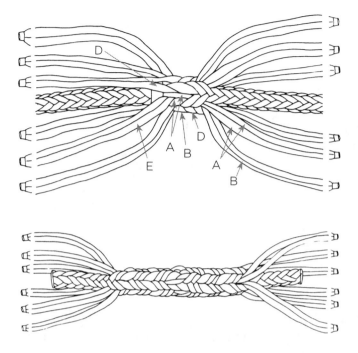

Complete another three rounds of tucks and taper again, this time by cutting one strand from each pair. Retape the ends.

Complete three more rounds of tucks with the three single strands. Then draw up the strand as you would a loose shoelace, until the pieces of the rope lay together but are not overly tight or loose.

Tape the ends, leaving a tail about 1½ inches (38 mm) long.

Whipping and Seizing

Both whipping and seizing are methods for binding rope, but whipping prevents the end of a rope from unlaying, while seizing binds two pieces of rope together, side by side. A traditional whipping is a tight winding of waxed or tarred small stuff; the more modern alternative is an application of one or two coats of a specially formulated liquid adhesive. Most marine supply stores carry these materials, often in kit form.

For seizing, many people now use plastic ties, which provide a quick, inexpensive way to bundle rope. Traditional seizing, however, looks good and will not damage or mark the rope.

TRADITIONAL WHIPPING

The width of the whipping should approximate the diameter of the rope. It is best to have two whippings a short distance apart—one near the rope end and one a few rope diameters farther up the standing part—with the small stuff pulled tight on each. If one is loosened, the other should keep the end from unlaying.

TOOLS & MATERIALS

Rope to be whipped
Small stuff: waxed whipping twine
Scissors or sharp knife
Vinyl tape
Hot knife or heat source

Tape the end of the rope or, if it is synthetic, heat-seal the end with a hot knife or other heat source until the yarns are fused.

Begin whipping at least an inch (25 mm) from the bitter end of the rope. Lay a loop of small stuff across the rope, leaving a tail of 5 or 6 inches (125 to 150 mm) on the bitter end. You will need to grasp this tail later, so don't cover the tail completely with whipping.

With the working piece of small stuff, wrap around the rope from the tail end toward the apex of the loop, covering the loop until the width of the whipping is at least as wide as the diameter of the rope.

To end the whipping, insert the working end of the small stuff through the loop. Pull on the bitter end, or tail, of the small stuff until the loop slides completely out of sight. Clip the ends close.

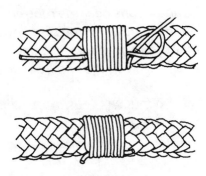

SAILMAKER'S WHIPPING

TOOLS & MATERIALS
Rope to be whipped
Small stuff: waxed whipping twine
Sailmaker's needle

Take two stitches through the rope with the small stuff to secure its end. Then wrap the small stuff around the rope, working back over the stitches, until the width of the whipping approximates the diameter of the rope.

Draw the working end of the small stuff under the entire length of the whipping and pull it through.

Now bring the small stuff over the whipping (left to right in the illustration) to make the first angled stitch. Stitch through about one-third of the rope's girth, staying on the same side of the whipping.

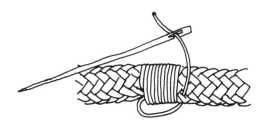

Rotate the rope 120 degrees. Bring the small stuff back across the whipping to make another angled stitch—parallel with the first, but one-third of the rope's circumference removed. Stitch through the rope again, and make a third angled stitch. Continue in this fashion until all the stitches are doubled, then clip the end.

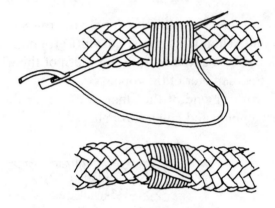

Note: For three-strand rope, the angled stitches follow the lay.

SEIZING

TOOLS & MATERIALS
Ropes to be seized
Nylon small stuff

The size and construction of the small stuff are your choice. Form a loop at the end of the small stuff and tuck the end two or three times through the lay of its standing part. If the ropes being seized are three-strand, work in the direction opposite the lay.

Circle the ropes to be seized, and anchor the working end of the small stuff by threading it through the loop and doubling it back upon itself. Apply eight to ten wraps around the ropes, taking care to cover the tail.

Take a hitch (as shown) and, working back across the seizing, place a layer of wraps over the first layer. These wraps are called *riding turns* because they "ride" on the first layer. The riding turns should not be as tight as the original turns and should number one fewer.

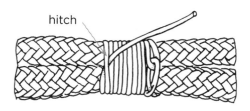

hitch

Pass the working end through the original loop and wrap two turns across the seizing, between the two ropes (see drawing next page); take up any slack.

Tie a Flat Knot (see illustration). Draw the knot tight and clip close.

CHAFE PROTECTION

Somewhere along the line between the magnificent sailing vessels of the mid-1800s and today, chafing gear on ropes has disappeared. And that's a shame because today's ropes, with their high-tech fiber blends and state-of-the-art construction, demand protection for more reasons than the twisted manila, linen, and cotton rigging of old.

Good synthetic ropes are expensive, but they do not rot away. If you choose your ropes carefully and spend a little extra time applying chafing gear where needed, you should get years of useful service from them. I can assure you that you'll save both money and worry.

Lengths of garden hose or vinyl tubing are often used as chafing sleeves on mooring and anchor lines and sometimes in rigging, but the methods described here provide a more handsome alternative.

For the sake of simplicity, let us assume you are purchasing new ropes with plans to add chafing gear to the eye and/or at a point of probable wear on the standing part—that is, any place where the rope will repeatedly rub against a hard surface or another rope.

One type of chafe sleeve is fashioned from the coat of a double-braid rope. I like to use this for chafe protection on three-strand, hollow-braid, and plaited ropes. (For chafe protection on double-braid, I prefer to use leather, for reasons given later.)

Buy a short piece of double-braid the same diameter as your rope to make the chafe sleeve. There is no hard-and-fast rule on how long to make the sleeve. Decide how much length you'll need for the eye; then add 3 or 4 inches (75 to 100 mm) to allow for raveling at the ends of the sleeve and for the tendency of the sleeve to "collapse"—or shrink lengthwise—when you slide it over the rope you are protecting.

Remove the core from the double-braid and tape the resultant sleeve loosely at both ends. Then tightly and smoothly tape the rope end over which you will be sliding the sleeve. To make the job easier, sew one end of a cord to the rope end, making the cord a little longer than the sleeve.

Run the other end of the cord through the sleeve, then carefully remove the tape at the ends of the sleeve. (The sleeve ends will unravel for an inch or two/25 to 50 mm.)

With the ends free, the sleeve will expand enough to allow the rope to be pulled through. Use the cord to fish the rope through the sleeve.

Once the sleeve is on the rope, re-tape the sleeve just inside its raveled ends. Position the sleeve on what will be the eye. Trim the ends of the sleeve close to the tape and apply a few extra wraps to reinforce the ends.

Now splice the eye following the directions given in other chapters.

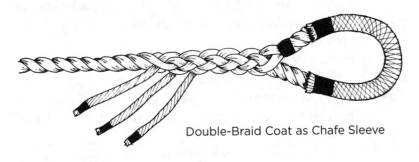

Double-Braid Coat as Chafe Sleeve

A leather chafe sleeve probably offers the best protection for both wire and fiber ropes, and I prefer this chafe protection for double-braid rope. Because there is a crossover step in the middle of the double-braid eye splice (see chapter 4), a sleeve would have to be applied in the middle of the splice; in all the confusion, it's easy to wind up with the sleeve either not on the rope at all or in the wrong place. The leather, on the other hand, can be wrapped and sewn after the eye is formed, and it looks better to boot.

Applying a leather sleeve can be complicated, but my instructions and a kit like the one manufactured by Sea-Dog (available from any marine store) will simplify the job. The kit will give you a piece of leather sized to the rope diameter you're covering, with holes prepunched along the mating edges. You also get needle, twine, and directions for sewing. (Unlike the chafe sleeve made out of double-braid, the leather sleeve is not moveable once it is applied, a fact that could be relevant when you're protecting a chafe-prone section of a standing part rather than an eye.)

Execute the double-braid eye splice almost to completion, stopping just short of the lock-stitch (see page 46). Mark the eye, then carefully "unmilk" the splice to expose the crossover. If the crossover is disturbed, the splice will be spoiled, so it is wise to stitch the crossover with needle and twine to prevent any slippage.

Unmilk the splice farther so that the marks on the core delineating the extent of the eye are in a straight line. Then put this straight-line section under tension with two lengths of small stuff, pulling in opposite directions. (Hitch the small stuff to the rope with timber hitches, as shown; see page 226 for a close-up view of the timber hitch.) A firm pull is all that is necessary. This will make the job easier because your hands will be free to hold the sleeve in place while you sew.

Keeping the seam to the outside of the eye and sewing as shown, wrap the leather sleeve according to the directions that come with the kit.

Release the rope and milk the splice back into place. It is not necessary to remove the stitches in the crossover.

Don't forget the last step, the lock-stitch (see page 46).

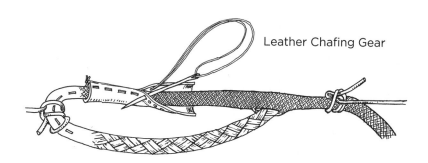

Leather Chafing Gear

You can, of course, use leather instead of a double-braid coat for chafe protection on twisted, plaited, and hollow-braid ropes as well. Make marks on the rope where the eye is to be, then apply the leather sleeve before you splice the eye. Put the marked section under tension with two timber-hitched lengths of small stuff pulling in opposite directions, thus freeing your hands to hold and sew the leather in place. Arrange the leather's seam so it lies on the outside of the eye. Release the rope from tension and complete the splice.

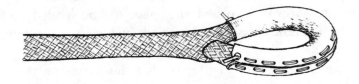

FOURTEEN

Sew-and-Serve Eye Splice

Served ropework lends an air of tradition and, for the owner of a traditional vessel, a few of these splices aboard would add a nice touch of the old days.

This splice works very well for double-braid, eight-plait, and twelve-plait rope. The splice requires a layer of serving; it is important that the sewing be very tight and the taper very smooth.

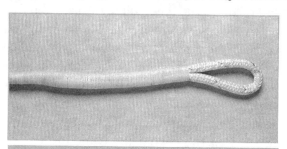

TOOLS & MATERIALS

Double-braid rope
Serving mallet or heaver
Whipping twine
Sharp knife

Lay out your line forming the necessary eye. For the length of the splice, allow seven or eight times the inside diameter of the eye.

Place a tight seizing at the throat, then remove the tape or melted tip from the end of the tail and taper the tail smoothly with an angled cut through the coat and core. The cut should terminate 3 to 5 inches (75 to 125 mm) back from the end.

Comb, coax, and stroke the coat strands until they straighten along the axis of the tail. The strands will become indistinct, blending with the core yarns in the taper.

Then "marl" down the tapered tail by firmly binding it to the standing part with a series of hitches. Start at the base of the tail, passing the twine through the heart of the standing part and putting a stopper knot in the end of the twine. Work away from the eye, toward the end of the taper, tying off the other end in any convenient fashion.

Sew the two lengths of rope together between the marling and the seizing. Pass the needle and twine through the centers of both lengths of line by turns, pulling the twine as taut as possible as you go. Begin the stitching just below the throat seizing; when you reach the marling, start right back the other way, creating cross-stitches as you go. Tie off the two ends at the throat with a square knot (see chapter 27).

marling

To set up the splice for serving, tie it up with a good strain, taut between two posts.

For serving, you'll need a serving tool, which dispenses small stuff in tighter turns than you can possibly achieve otherwise, or a serving mallet, the traditional alternative (see the heaver illustration in chapter 1 and on page 136).

Start the serving at the throat with twine and the mallet. After burying the end of the waxed twine beneath the first several turns, proceed with the serving until the entire splice is smoothly and tightly covered.

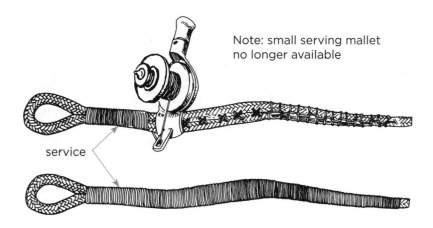

Note: small serving mallet
no longer available

service

Allow only the last six or seven wraps to remain loose. Reeve the end of the twine back under the slack turns, snug the turns as tightly as possible, and cut the end close.

The design of an arborist style heaver or serving mallet is radically different from that of the sailor's standard serving mallet. At no time are any of the turns of the service out of sight because they are under the barrel of the standard mallet.

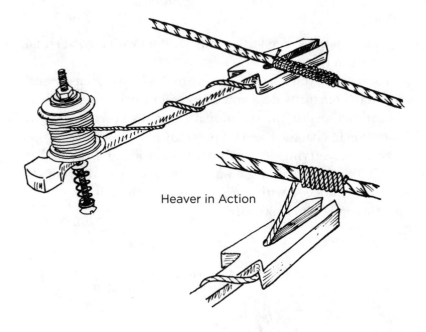

Heaver in Action

PART TWO

SPLICING WIRE ROPE

Introduction to Wire Rope

"When you have completed as many wire splices as you are old, you will be ready."

—Peter Klenk

L ore has it that wire rope was first used in the mines in Germany, where even the best-crafted plant fiber ropes failed quickly. Wilhelm Albert is credited with the first official wire rope walk there in 1831. Subsequent history of wire rope is a bit unclear. I've heard that John A. Roebling, a graduate engineer of Berlin, emigrated from Germany to America with a diagram of Albert's wire rope walk in his pocket. Another source indicates that Roebling found an obscure paper on how to set up and run a wire rope walk, and that by 1841 he had set up a wire rope walk in Germantown, Pennsylvania.

Before the U.S. Civil War, embers from the fires powering steamships often drifted aloft, catching fiber riggings on fire, so slowly fiber rigging was replaced by wire. During the Civil War mariners discovered that steel rigging had the added benefit of resisting enemy cannon fire, keeping boats intact and afloat longer than they would have with traditional fiber rigging. After the war, wire rope found its way onto steel suspension bridges and telegraph wires.

Today wire serves many purposes—from cables holding highway guardrails to wires supporting the telephone pole outside your window. The aircraft and logging industries use a great deal of wire, and the boating world does too. Sailing dinghies use the smallest diameter wire rope to hold their masts aloft, powerboats use wire steering cables, and large fishing draggers use wire to connect their immense trawls to their boats.

WIRE CHOICES FOR BOATS

Wire rope is made up of wire strands in groups (twisted) circling a core of soft fiber or hard steel and is available in galvanized and stainless steel. Wire rope is used in slings, winch ropes, and guy wires and is also acceptable for shrouds and stays. The term *aircraft cable* sometimes refers to wire rope, but indicates that the wire has been constructed with special strength for the aircraft industry. Wire rope is often offered with a coating of white plastic for lifelines.

Use is a prime consideration when choosing wire. A steering cable, for example, should be made of the finest stainless steel available and be as flexible as possible, because it is in constant motion. Shrouds, on the other hand, should be strong but not necessarily flexible, because they stay in one position.

Any wire used on a boat, whether it's aircraft cable or wire rope, needs to resist corrosion. Stainless steel wire is an alloy of steel, chromium, and nickel. Type 316 is the most resistant to corrosion (followed by 305, then 302/304) and is used in high-corrosive atmospheres such as the Gulf of Mexico and the Caribbean, where salt spray is highly potent. Galvanized wire, known as plough steel in Europe, is made of carbon steel that has been dipped in a hot bath of zinc and is stronger than stainless steel wire. Country of origin makes a difference in the quality of any metal. Some U.S. suppliers no longer sell wire products manufactured offshore.

Wire Identification

A typical identification for wire might look like this: ⅛-inch (3 mm) 7 × 19 316 stainless.

Three parameters are indicated:

1. The diameter of the wire, usually in inches, e.g., ⅛ inch (3 mm), ⁵⁄₃₂ inch (4 mm), and ³⁄₁₆ inch (5 mm). Boat wire is available in sizes from ³⁄₃₂ inch (2 mm) to ⁷⁄₁₆ inch (11 mm) and beyond.
2. Two numbers referring to the wire's construction (e.g., 7 × 19)—see below.
3. The type of material, e.g., 316 stainless steel.

No matter the construction—1 × 19, 7 × 7, or 7 × 19—the more strands a bundle has, the more flexible the rope. So, for instance, 1 × 19 wire rope, a common choice for standing rigging because it's stiff, is a one-strand cable made of 19 wires twisted together. Viewed from the end, the arrangement of the wires looks like a flower; one wire forms the center, six wires surround that, and twelve wires form the outer circle.

Standing rigging is often constructed of 1 × 19 stainless wire rope. (Loos)

Wire terminology is subtle. Riggers and manufacturers often use terms interchangeably and differently. For example, 1 × 19 wire rope differs from 7 × 19 flexible wire, which is commonly used for halyards and contains seven strands, or bundles, of 19 wires each. Each bundle is constructed like the 1 × 19 wire rope described above. One bundle forms the center of 7 × 19 wire and is surrounded by six identically constructed bundles.

Wire halyards are often constructed of 7 × 19 flexible stainless wire. (Loos)

There is also 7 × 7 lanyard wire, which consists of a center bundle of seven wires surrounded by six bundles of seven wires.

Lifelines are often constructed of 7 × 7 flexible wire. (Loos)

The last parameter is the type and quality of the metal used in the manufacture of the wire: type 302/304 (commercial grade) stainless steel, type 316 (corrosion-resistant) stainless steel, galvanized wire, and so on.

A note on measurements: when you buy coated wire for lifelines, you will often find two diameters. The first is the base diameter of the wire itself and the second is the base diameter plus the coating.

Wire configurations that are the most commonly found on boats are listed below.

Stainless Steel and/or Galvanized
- 1 × 19 wire rope (nonflexible, standing rigging, also for guying applications)
- 1 × 7 wire rope (nonflexible, in small sizes for fishing leaders and lines)
- 7 × 7 stainless steel wire (lanyard wire, often used in lifelines)
- 7 × 7 galvanized wire
- 7 × 19 flexible wire, used for halyards
- 7 × 16
- 6 × 25 IWRC (Independent Wire Rope Core)

Types of Galvanized Wire
- ⅝-inch (16 mm) blue galvanized combination wire (This combines synthetic rope with a wire heart and is used only for splicing training or on fishing boats.)
- ⅝-inch (16 mm) 6 × 17 galvanized wire, lightly greased

- ⁹⁄₁₆-inch (14 mm) 6 × 17 galvanized wire
- ⁹⁄₃₂-inch (7 mm) 1 × 19 stainless steel

Alternate Rigging Materials

There are other, specialized materials, mostly found on high-tech boats. One brand is Dyform, which is a specially constructed type of stainless steel wire that carries greater strength for less weight. Materials used in standing rigging include rod (stainless), Kevlar, PBO (Zylon, which is a polymer), and Vectran (also a polymer).

Four Boats and Their Rigging Wire

The four examples that follow illustrate the use of wire in boat rigging.

Two Eagles is a 19-foot (6 m) fiberglass Bristol built in 1978 in Bristol, Rhode Island. She carries a fractional marconi rig, with stays and shrouds of ³⁄₁₆-inch (5 mm) 1 × 19 stainless steel with swaged forks and eyes. Her topping lift is ¹⁄₁₆-inch (1.5 mm) 7 × 19 stainless steel. Her running rigging is all fiber rope, and there are no lifelines. The builder designed and installed her rigging, and since then the owner has not changed the hull or mast. Should the rigging need replacing, all the owner would do is call the factory in Bristol.

Next is *Sea Fire*, a Crocker 30.6 (#267). She is a full-keel wooden boat designed by Sam Crocker and built in Manchester, Massachusetts, in 1952 by Crocker's son. *Sea Fire* is marconi rigged, with stays and shrouds of ⁹⁄₃₂-inch (7 mm) 1 × 19 stainless steel with swaged forks and eyes. Two stays of ¼-inch (6 mm) 1 × 19 are under the bow pulpit and two stays of the same size hold the boomkin (the aft spar). Her running backstays are ⁵⁄₃₂-inch (4 mm) 7 × 19 stainless steel. (Note that the diameter measurement includes the coating on the wires, which protects against chafe on the sails.) Her lifelines are ⁷⁄₁₆-inch (11 mm) stainless steel coated with white vinyl (most lifelines I've seen are 1 × 19 stainless steel), and the forks and eyes on her lifelines and running backstays are swaged. The outhaul on the mainsail boom is ⅛-inch (3 mm) 7 × 19 stainless steel.

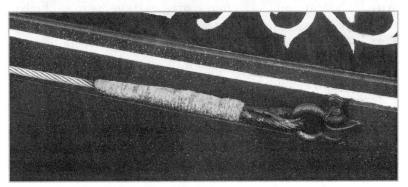

Even if you never splice a wire on your boat, careful inspection of all wire and splices (as well as the parceling and service protecting those splices) should be part of your routine maintenance. (Molly Mulhern)

Over the years, the owner has made changes to *Sea Fire*. He lengthened her pulpit to allow for a different foresail, and he added running backstays. He called on Tim Witten of Bristol, Rhode Island, to rig the boat. Tim is an experienced and knowledgeable rigger who, after discussing and studying pictures and plans, matched the existing rigging. The work was performed in my shop. A beginner at the time, I was happy to let Tim take the lead while I did all the splicing and swaging.

Elizabeth Helen is a 65-foot (20 m) western-rig steel fishing boat. Her owner fishes out of Point Judith, Rhode Island, for squid, herring, and flounder. A day boat, her rigging is ¾-inch (19 mm) galvanized, and her paravanes are ⁹⁄₁₆-inch (14 mm) galvanized. The fittings are swaged hard eyes shackled straight to pad eyes on the deck.

The fourth vessel is the beautiful 38-foot (12 m) gaff-rigged schooner *Winfield Lash*. The owner commissioned Lash Boatyard in Friendship, Maine, to build the boat's hull. He completed the vessel in his backyard and commissioned Brion Toss to rig her. Toss hand spliced and served all the wire rigging in traditional fashion.

INSPECTING AND CARING FOR WIRE

Wire on boats is subject to many stresses, ranging from the corrosiveness of salt air to the pressure caused by pounding and rolling seas. The insides of wire terminals and barrel fittings can collect water, leading to corrosion. Wire rope is sneaky—corrosion can hide, becoming evident only *after* a rig has toppled. Use a magnifying glass to really see what's going on—small cracks

> **SAFETY TIP**
> *Working with wire is hazardous. First and foremost, always wear safety glasses. Gloves help prevent cuts and abrasions, and an apron protects your clothing and chest.*

are places where water can enter, so pay attention to them. Once the outer coating of stainless is breached, rusting and pitting can begin. If you see that in your rigging wire, attend to it swiftly. Inspect shrouds for bends in the wires and frayed ends, picturesquely named "meat hooks." Most sailboat rigs should not be considered strong if they are older than ten years.

To get the most life out of your wire, use the correct hardware (your assembly is only as strong as its weakest link) and keep wires free of salt by dousing with fresh water after the day's sailing. Replace any service that comes apart or unwrapped. (For more on the importance of service to the life of wire see the chapter on Lizards, page 175.)

Splicing will improve both the longevity and strength of your wire. However, a correctly placed and pressed swage is acceptable. Some splices are not meant to carry a load for long—don't use the Tugboat Splice (also known as a Flemish Eye or Molly Hogan; see page 160) in situations that call for a permanent splice.

WORKING WITH WIRE

In addition to being dangerous (see safety precautions opposite), working with wire can be difficult. Heavy wires are challenging to work with—an assistant is a great help. Wire can spring and jump when unwound from a coil, so proceed with caution. Set up your work area so there is plenty of clearance around the vise—especially behind you—so the wire can run out straight and true. Kinks in any kind of wire can't be undone and permanently diminish the wire strength.

Tools and Materials for Working with Wire

Many of the tools used for wire splicing are also used in fiber and rope splicing. Shown here are three setups for different rigging jobs, ranging from a traditional rigging made with seizings of pine tar to materials used on a modern yacht rig. In addition to safety glasses and gloves (leather or robust neoprene), you'll

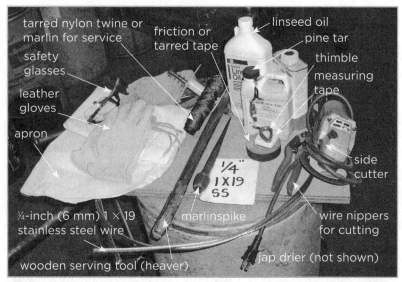

tarred nylon twine or marlin for service

friction or tarred tape

linseed oil

pine tar

safety glasses

thimble

measuring tape

leather gloves

apron

side cutter

1/4" 1 X 19 SS

¼-inch (6 mm) 1 × 19 stainless steel wire

marlinspike

wire nippers for cutting

wooden serving tool (heaver)

jap drier (not shown)

Use these materials when the wire splicing will be seized in a traditional fashion (see page 127 for instructions). Note that tarred nylon twine shrinks when wet or hot. Also, I prefer wooden measuring sticks over measuring tape, but they're hard to find these days. The wire shown here can also be used on any modern sailboat.

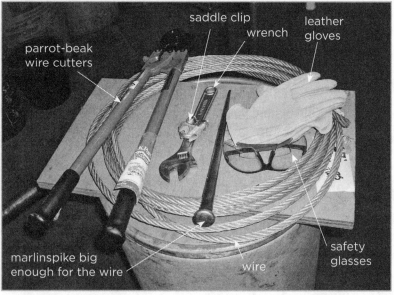

saddle clip

wrench

leather gloves

parrot-beak wire cutters

marlinspike big enough for the wire

wire

safety glasses

Material for a Tugboat Splice (see page 160) with no service.

Another selection of materials needed for wire splicing, with the addition of the vise in the background.

need a vise, wire cutters, a side cutter (which can be used instead of nippers), a steel marlinspike (a stout screwdriver might do in a pinch), a wrench, pliers, and, if doing a more traditional rigging job, materials for seizings (including a serving tool).

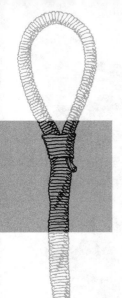

SIXTEEN

Liverpool Wire Splice

The instructions here are for a basic 7 × 19 "soft-eye" splice that can be used as a lizard (which works like a bungee cord) for a temporary fairlead. The ⅜-inch-diameter (9 mm) 7 × 19 is easy to work with; if you haven't made this splice before, use galvanized wire, which is less springy than stainless steel. Stick to a soft-eye splice (no thimble) until you get the hang of this wire splice: a thimble makes the eye harder to keep in the vise.

The splice is shown here with a tight service through the whole eye area. This protects you by preventing the individual strands from shifting and popping the eye out of the vise while you're making the splice, and it ultimately protects the wire from weather and early wear. The strands of a wire bent into a curve become compressed or flattened on the outside edge of the curve. This distortion causes the wire to lose strength. Service corsets the wire, holding it to its rounder shape and protecting the splice and eye from moisture.

TOOLS & MATERIALS

6 feet (1.8 m) of ⅜ inch (9 mm) 7 × 19 wire
"Parrot-beak"-style and
diagonal wire cutters
Rigging vise and marlinspike
Tarred tape or friction tape
Pine tar or some water-repelling mixture
40 feet (12 m) of tarred twine or marlin
Sharp knife
Marking pen
Vinyl tape
Safety glasses

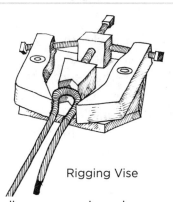

Rigging Vise

Pictured here is a small rigging vise (see photo on page 156, too). Made by Mr. Z (available at auctions, marine flea markets, and marine antique stores), it's bronze and measures 4 × 5 inches (100 × 125 mm). It's adjustable three ways by turning the screws. For fine-tuning or tightening, it's a good idea to have a wrench close by. The rigging vise's only purpose is to aid splicing stranded wire in sizes from the smallest to ⅜ inch (9 mm).

Here's how to start. On your length of wire, mark a spot 2 feet (600 mm) up from the working end (mark 1, below). From that spot, apply pine tar or water-repellent coating toward the working end for a distance of about 7 inches (175 mm). Working back toward mark 1, wrap a layer of tarred tape over the tar. Then wrap the service, which becomes your eye, working from mark 1 toward the working end, against the lay of the wire.

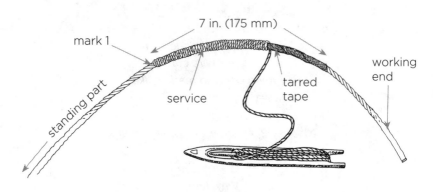

Clamp your wire in the vise the "right way," literally. To do this, stand facing the vise with the wire bent in your hand. The working end of the wire—the 2-foot (600 mm) end—should be in your right hand; the standing part should be in your left. Now put your piece in the vise and clamp it down. During splicing, you'll probably want to stand on the left side of your work.

On the working end, unlay all the strands and tape the ends.

Insert the marlinspike into the wire at the marked point from left to right, as shown opposite in A (mark 1). Take care to go over the top of the heart, or core, of the standing part and pick up only three strands of the standing part. Now rotate the marlinspike one full circle down the wire around the heart of the standing part, as if the spike were a sort of propeller with the wire as its hub. The spike will travel down the wire from position 1 to position 3. Leave the marlinspike stuck through the wire.

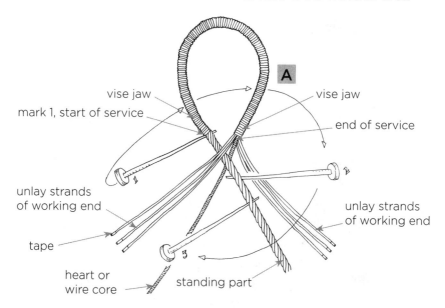

Put on safety glasses and bring Strand 1, the innermost strand of the working part (the one that nearly "kisses" mark 1) into position so it lies on top of the standing part at mark 1 (B). Then bring Strand 1 completely under the standing part and make a gentle turn in the strand so you can tuck it back through the space made by the marlinspike, right to left, at position 3.

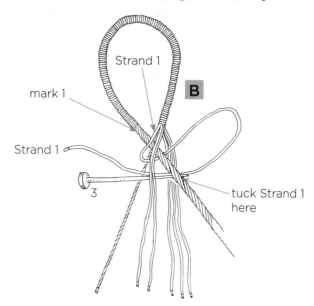

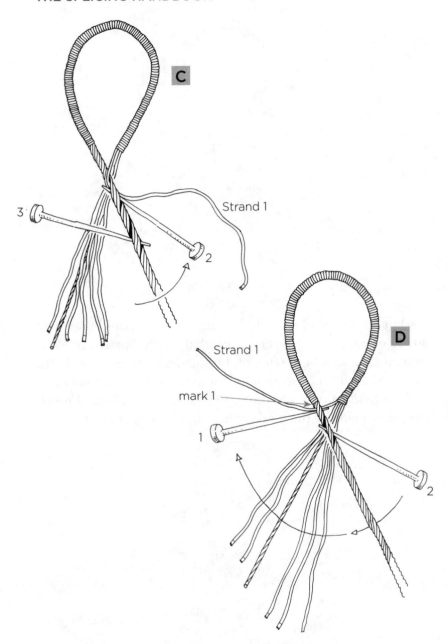

Roll the spike back from position 3 (C) to the start of the service (mark 1), position 1 in (D), and simultaneously gently pull back the slack out of the wire.

Insert the marlinspike over the heart at mark 1 (D) and pick up only two strands of the standing part this time. Rotate the marlinspike as before so it travels down the wire. Insert Strand 2 (the strand next to Strand 1) of the working end at the same place as Strand 1, but exit the standing part one strand farther away from the beginning of the service (mark 1). Roll the spike back, close to mark 1. With Strand 3, pick up only one strand. Remember to have it enter at the same spot as Strands 1 and 2.

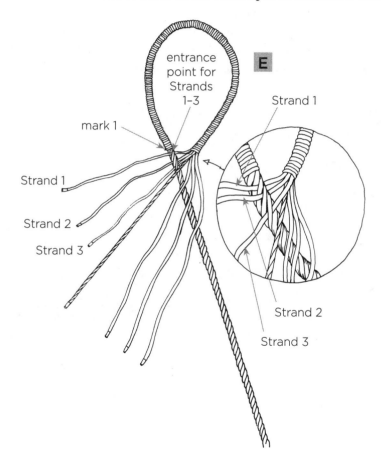

To hold your work in place, use the marlinspike to tuck Strand 3 five more times. As you rotate the marlinspike down the wire, wind the working strand around the wire *with* the lay, always tucking Strand 3 under the same working strand.

Now we have to bury the heart of the working end. Insert the marlinspike in the same spot where Strand 3 was first tucked, and set the heart across the wire and behind the spike (inset A in drawing F). This motion or method is different from tucking. For lack of a better description, we're going to pry the heart of the working end into the center around the heart of the standing end for several inches. You'll get the knack pretty quickly because the wire will bind your tool if you're doing it the wrong way. Another thing: if your work is looking a lot different from the examples, don't be so quick to blame yourself; there is a ton of poor-quality wire for sale these days. Bury the heart of the working end for about 18 inches (450 mm) and tape it so it can't spring out (G).

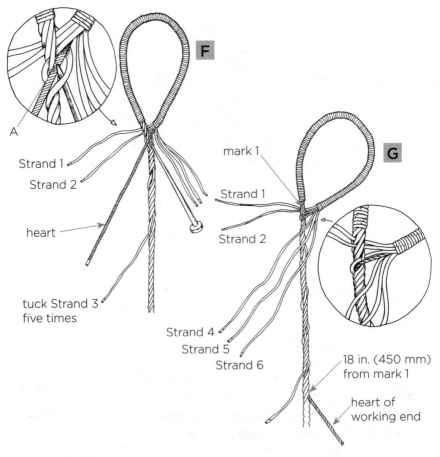

A

Strand 1

Strand 2

heart

tuck Strand 3
five times

F

mark 1

Strand 1

Strand 2

G

Strand 4

Strand 5

Strand 6

18 in. (450 mm)
from mark 1

heart of
working end

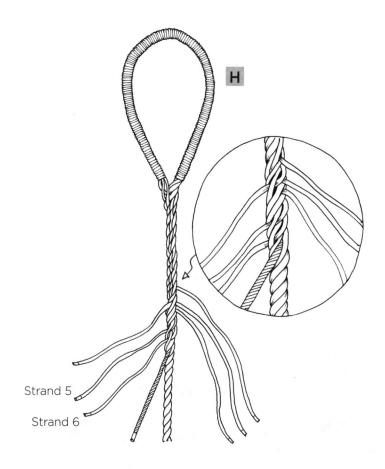

Strand 5

Strand 6

To tuck Strand 4, put the spike in the same space into which the heart went, picking up just one strand. Tuck Strand 4 six times. Pick up the next strand down (Strand 5) and tuck it six times. Finally, using the next strand down on the standing part of the wire, do the same with Strand 6. Now go back to the beginning and tuck Strands 1 and 2 each about five more times. It'll be hard to keep track of how many tucks you've made on an individual strand, but don't worry about it. It makes a better splice if the strands exit at different points, which creates a tapered splice. Clip off the wire tails close with the diagonal cutters.

Apply your service as described earlier in this chapter, starting at the base of the splice and working up to the eye. Now remove the finished and serviced splice from the rigging vise.

LOCK TUCK FOR LIVERPOOL WIRE SPLICE

The Liverpool Wire Eye Splice is the splice of choice for all "7 ×" wires, perfect for hoisting or lifting loads. However, if the splice is incomplete (without a tight jacket of service) and suspended with a load, it will gradually untwist and eventually drop its load. If the service comes off because of wear or age or because it wasn't applied well to begin with, the Liverpool splice might not hold. Setting in the two extra tucks shown here will prevent the Liverpool splice from coming apart.

TOOLS & MATERIALS
⁹⁄₁₆-inch (14 mm) blue
combination galvanized wire
Rigging vise
Marlinspike
Vinyl tape
Appropriate wire cutters
Safety glasses
Leather gloves

The ideal material for learning to splice wire is the ⁹⁄₁₆-inch (14 mm) 6 × 17 blue galvanized combination wire rope used on fishing trawlers. It's flexible enough to splice with your fingers. The center strand is straight and thick, and each strand that encircles it is wrapped in polypropylene.

heart is galvanized wire rope

these strands are wrapped in polypro

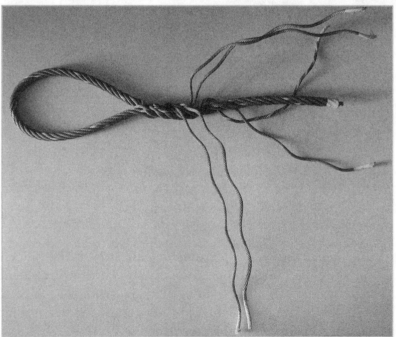

Liverpool splice in progress using blue galvanized wire. (Molly Mulhern)

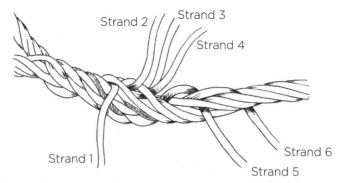

Strand 2 Strand 3
Strand 4
Strand 1
Strand 6
Strand 5

Strands 5 and 6 are tucked and ready to be trimmed.

After you complete a standard Liverpool Wire Splice and bury the heart (not shown in the illustration), but before you clip the wire ends, choose one of the six wire ends farthest away from the eye (Strand 6 in the illustration). Tuck the end under one strand by moving the spike in a U-turn *back against the lay*. Tuck the next wire end (Strand 5) under two strands. Continue with the next end, burying it under three strands.

Cut the ends off and smooth the splice in the usual manner.

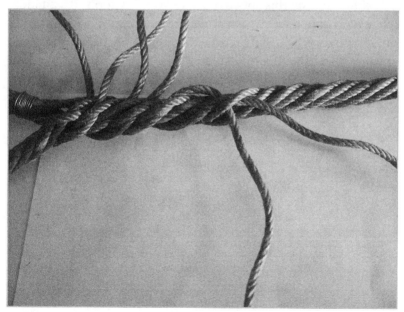

Close up view of lock tuck in process using galvanized wire.

SEVENTEEN

Tugboat Splice

Here's a simple wire splice that also goes by two other commonly known names: the Molly Hogan and the Flemish Eye. Since setting this splice requires very few tools, it's an ideal splice for a quick, temporary repair. It's commonly used in static situations, such as when landscapers need to hold trees in place or when telephone linemen need to anchor telephone poles and towers temporarily. I've seen highway guardrails that are held in place with this splice—but that is not an appropriate use of it. Never use this splice for anything beyond a temporary hold—in fact, several states have outlawed its use altogether!

TOOLS & MATERIALS

$\frac{7}{16}$-inch (11 mm) 6 × 25 IWRC
galvanized wire

Marlinspike

Saddle (cable) clip and wrench

Wire cutters

Rigging vise (optional)

Safety glasses

Gloves

When working with this wire, use great care to avoid injury; the ends of the wire are sharp. Clean off the ends, and then bend the wire back on itself to the size splice you want. Unlay three outside wires to a length twice the size of the eye you wish to create; to create a 6-inch (150 mm) eye, for example, unlay 12 inches (300 mm) of the wire.

Wire unlaid into two bundles of three wires each. The heart is in the bundle on the right.

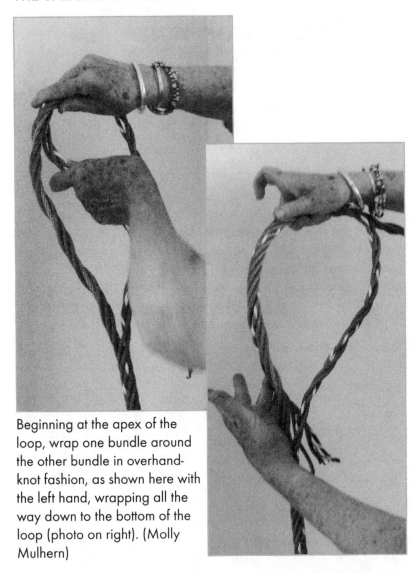

Beginning at the apex of the loop, wrap one bundle around the other bundle in overhand-knot fashion, as shown here with the left hand, wrapping all the way down to the bottom of the loop (photo on right). (Molly Mulhern)

At the apex of the loop, pass the free end of one bundle through the loop like you would if you were tying an overhand knot. Repeating this maneuver again and again, spiral or grapevine *both* bundles down the two sides of the splice until they meet at the throat.

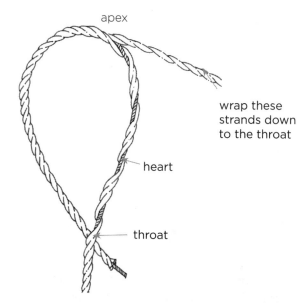

apex

wrap these
strands down
to the throat

heart

throat

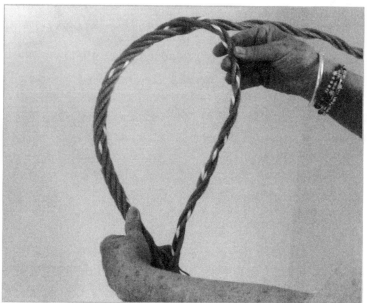

Wrapping is complete on the left side, but the tail of wires heading
off at the loop's apex (in both the photo and the illustration) indicates that the wire on the right side of the loop needs to be spiraled
down to the throat. (Molly Mulhern)

If the lengths of the bundles are correct, there should be just enough to gather up the ends with a saddle clip at the throat. Should there be a lot of excess, it's not hard to undo the ends and adjust the lengths to fit.

Clipping the ends with a saddle clip can be difficult. The splice is easy enough to unlay and rewrap if you have time. Unclipped ends are dangerous.

This splice should never be used in a manner that may cause harm to life and limb.

EIGHTEEN
Lap Wire Splice

A s the name suggests, two wires are laid end to end, over-lapped. The fiber rope counterpart of this splice is called an End-to-End Splice (see the several end-to-end splices earlier in this book). To create an End-to-End Splice, we remove the tape or melted ends of the ropes, unlay the ends to a particular length, interlace or "marry" the tails, and finally splice the ropes with six full rounds of tucks. The similarity between the End-to-End Splice and the Lap Wire Splice ends, however, after the first step—removing the tape from the end of the wire, if there is tape there.

The Lap Wire Splice is used to repair a broken or damaged section of rope or to add length. First one end is unlaid and spliced (Liverpool-style) into its partner. The whole job is turned, and the second end is unlaid and spliced. The nature of the double splice prevents any unlaying action. Also, very often the splice is set in quickly.

Note that the splice pictured here has not been served. Service should be applied as soon after splicing as possible, to avoid injury caused by sharp ends.

Use plain ⅝-inch (16 mm) galvanized wire with a fiber core

soaked in oil and coated with grease. You'll want to clean the area to be spliced with solvent (denatured alcohol), using gloves and rags to protect your hands from the rough wire ends.

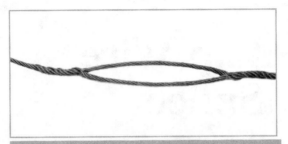

TOOLS & MATERIALS

⅝-inch (16 mm) 6 × 17 galvanized
wire, lightly greased

Rigging vise

Marlinspike

Denatured alcohol

Parrot-beak cutters and grinder

Unlaying stick

Serving mallet with material

Tarred tape and #30 tarred nylon

Seizing wire and thimble

Marking pen and tape

Apron and shop rags

Gloves

Safety glasses

Lay out the wires side by side, as shown, to mark the areas where the splices will go. As a rule of thumb, for ½-inch (12 mm) wire, the length of tails for this splice is 18 inches (450 mm). At

apply seizing

tail

tail

18 in. (450 mm)

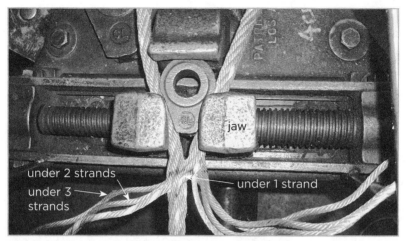

Place the wires in the vise with the jaws at the seizing you marked in the first step (the seizings are not shown in this photo).

the 18-inch (450 mm) spots, mark the two wires and apply seizings (see page 166).

Arrange the wires in the vise. Set the thimble in the middle and tighten the jaws of the vise so they hold the wires securely.

Separate the strands and apply a standard Liverpool Wire Splice (see page 148).

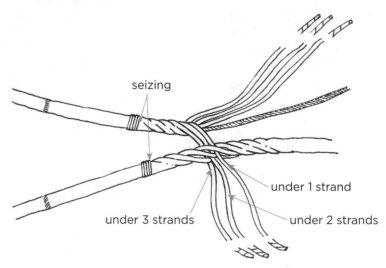

For the sake of clarity, the beginnings of the Liverpool Wire Splice are shown here without the vise.

After finishing your tucks and cutting off the strands, pound (gently at first) the splice with the mallet and, if necessary, smooth ragged ends with the grinder or side-cutting tool. Apply a layer of tarred tape to act as parceling. Turn the wires around and once again set them in the vise. This end is executed the same way as the first, with a standard Liverpool Wire Splice.

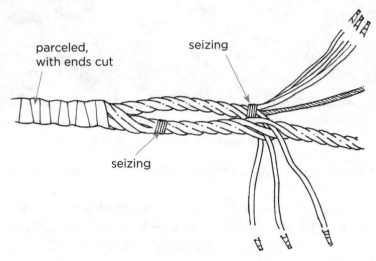

One side of this Lap Wire Splice has been completed, seized, and parceled. On the other side, the first three strands have been tucked.

Completely cover both ends of the finished Lap Wire Splice with parceling.

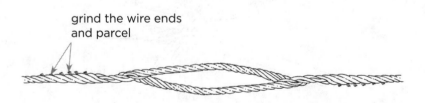

The wire ends of this splice have not been ground, nor have the sides of the splice been parceled.

NINETEEN

Mill Valley Splice

I f the Liverpool Wire Splice (page 148) is the king of wire splicing, the Mill Valley Splice is the queen. Like the Tugboat Splice
(page 160), it is used in static situations, serving as stays aboard
ship, for example. This is a challenging splice and not readily done

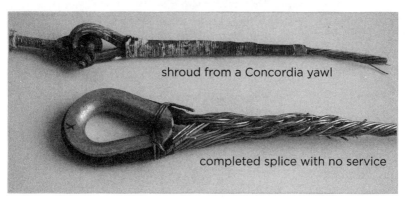

shroud from a Concordia yawl

completed splice with no service

The Mill Valley Splice has a long history, but is not an easy splice.
Here, a Mill Valley Splice (top) found on a Concordia yawl is
displayed next to a more recent Mill Valley Splice shown before its
final service with tarred nylon. Note the seizing under the thimble.
(Molly Mulhern)

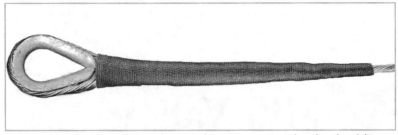

A completed Mill Valley Splice, without seizing under the thimble.

anywhere but in a rigging shop by professional riggers. Because of its stiff and springy nature, it can be difficult to work. I recommend that you have some experience with the Liverpool Wire Splice and are comfortable with it before attempting this one.

The splice described here is made with $\frac{9}{32}$-inch (7 mm) 1 × 9 stainless, left lay. Note that it's served with fiber (tarred nylon) rather than wire.

Use the best stainless steel wire available—I don't remember if this one was done with #302 (a softer wire) or #316. It's rated to break at 7,725 pounds (3500 kg). When tested, the splice attained 88 percent of the breaking strength—an excellent result.

TOOLS & MATERIALS
$\frac{9}{32}$-inch (7 mm) 1 × 19 stainless steel wire
Wire vise
Marlinspike
Serving mallet with #48 tarred nylon twine
Seizing wire and thimble
Japan drier
Linseed oil
Pine tar
Tarred tape
Parrot-beak cutters
Grinder
Unlaying stick
Wood mallet
Marking pen and tape

First apply a tight service around the eye. Keep in mind that the wire thimble must be able to accept the extra width the service adds. Set your work in the vise. If the eye is a soft one, use the thimble and seizing wire to hold the piece in place. Allow 18 inches (450 mm) for the tails.

Unlay the end by separating the outer wires into groups of two. Choose carefully, as these pairs need to be made up from strands that are right next to each other. Now unlay the core wires—match each pair of outer wires with a single core wire that's closest. If there is a center wire, leave it by itself (wire center not shown in our illustrations).

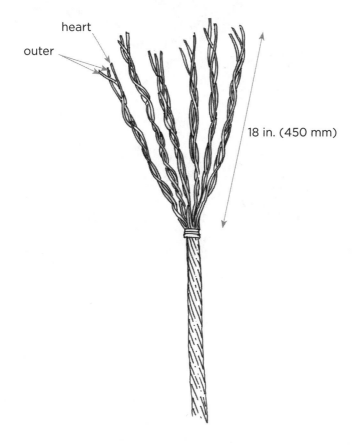

heart

outer

18 in. (450 mm)

The ends have been separated into groups. The seizing has not yet been wrapped around the area that will go into the thimble.

Tuck in the first group of strands under four wires. You may find it helpful to use an unlaying stick from here on. The next group of strands is tucked under two wires (see the illustration).

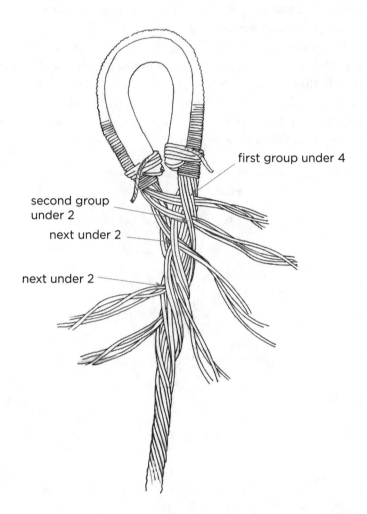

first group under 4

second group
under 2

next under 2

next under 2

Insert the next set of wires under two (to the left). If there is a center (not shown in our art), bring the center wire into the middle of the splice. Working wire strands in 1 × 19 are inclined to pop out, so tape or tie this one in place. Finish tucking the remaining groups of wires.

Completing the tucks.

Work all the tucked wires up and as close as possible to the thimble. Seize the area to prevent the wires from slipping or loosening (see page 127 for instructions). Complete another round of tucks. Again, seize your work to keep the wires in place. (Molly Mulhern)

In the next round of tucks, one wire will remain out, which accomplishes two things: the splice will begin to taper, and one more round of tucks will be completed. Complete the round of tucks, leaving the center wire (if there is one) out of the splice. Do the last round of tucks. Cut the wires close and pound the splice gently until you're sure the cut ends don't pop out.

Remove the seizing and check to see that the individual wire ends are cut close. It might be necessary to smooth them further with a grinder or a side cutter.

Serve the spliced area tightly.

The sharp ends of the strand here will be less dangerous once they are ground down and serviced. (Molly Mulhern)

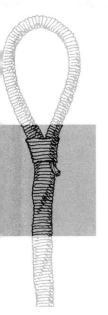

TWENTY

Lizards

For 30 years I've worked in boatyards, rigging and providing consulting services. I've developed a healthy sense of awe for the forces involved in staying a mast or sheeting in a mainsail, and a lively imagination for disasters that can result when those forces are unleashed on inadequate rigging.

So when I see the peculiar strategies and solutions some people use aboard otherwise impeccably turned-out boats, I'm shocked. One summer I was browsing the deck of a gold-plater docked in Newport, Rhode Island. It had perfectly finished teak decks, brightwork that didn't stop, bronze hardware, the works.

Right in the middle of all this, however—like a snake in boat paradise—was a rubber shock cord. I generally don't judge people by this stuff, but seeing a rubber shock cord aboard this floating theme park of fine boatbuilding was like being served a side of Marshmallow Fluff at an upscale restaurant.

This wasn't just a matter of aesthetics—the shock cords were unsuitable for the task at hand, serving as temporary fairleads to get the jibsheets around some boxes secured on the forward deck. Shock cords are untrustworthy, especially when used as

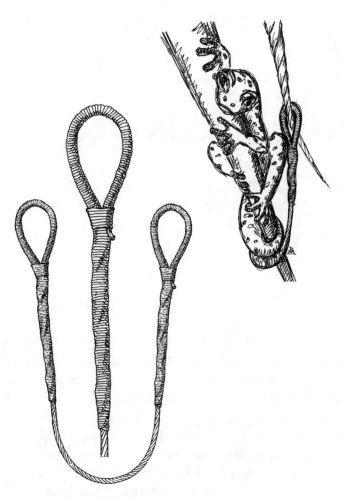

fairleads for vibrating loads, because they may unhook as they jiggle back and forth.

The Lizard not only looks better and works better, some consider it the perfect solution for tricky problems in the fairlead and lashing department. It also has the honorable pedigree that classic boat folks like.

Simply defined (by Gershom Bradford in *The Mariner's Dictionary*), a Lizard is "a piece of rope with a thimble or a bull's eye spliced in one end." Some sailors call it a strop, while others call it a pendant (and yet pronounce them "pennants"). How the term *lizard* came into it, I haven't yet found out.

Historically, Lizards have been used to steady a line or to give a sheet a change of direction. When used as a temporary expedient, they were tightly lashed in place. As a more permanent fixture, one end or eye was often large enough to fit around the mast. Small Lizards were used on the fittings of iron works or tied to the shroud to control a halyard. The British, never lacking in nautical imagination, sometimes called Lizards "jewel blocks." Bradford notes that jewel blocks and halyards in combination served the "lugubrious purpose" of reeving the rope by which men were hanged on naval ships.

In that golden age, Lizards were made with quality hemp cordage, as wire didn't make its debut until the middle of the nineteenth century. Here, I provide instructions for making a stainless-steel Lizard.

TOOLS & MATERIALS

4 feet (1.2 m) of 7 × 19 stainless steel wire
7-inch (175 mm) parrot-beak wire cutters
Tarred electrical or friction tape
40 feet (12.2 m) of #18 tarred nylon
Bench vise
*Marlinspike (for this size wire
a small awl will do)*
Sharp knife or scissors
Felt-tipped marking pen
Vinyl tape
Gel-type superglue
Safety glasses

Mark a spot 1 foot (300 mm) from one end of the stainless steel wire. (We'll call this section of wire the standing part.) Apply service this way: Starting at the 1-foot (300 mm) mark and continuing to about 6 inches (150 mm) from the other end, cover the wire with tarred electrical tape or friction tape, running with the lay of the wire (see art page 178). (Note that bare wire should be painted with a water-repellent coating such as pine tar, but for this project that step is optional.)

Next wrap a layer of tarred nylon *against* the lay of the wire. Secure the ends of the nylon as you would on a standard whipping (see page 123).

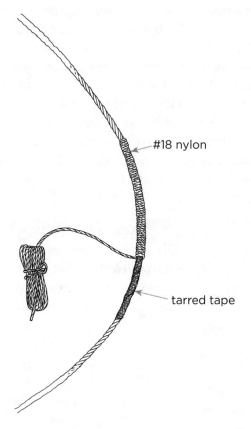

#18 nylon

tarred tape

When you bend a length of wire into a curve, the strands on the outer edge of the curve stretch a little, while the strands on the inner edge of the curve are slightly compressed or compacted. In other words, the wire—which is more or less cylindrical in cross section—tends to flatten. This action causes the wire to lose strength. Service acts like a corset of sorts, maintaining the wire's roundness and protecting the spliced area against moisture and rust for a longer period of time.

With your left hand, hold the end point of the service on the standing part of the wire. With your right hand, grasp the wire just below where the service ends. Bend the wire into a teardrop shape and watch to see which strand from the running end touches which strand on the standing part. This strand from the running end will be the first to run through the body of the wire, as close as possible to the service, passing *over* the heart or center strand. Don't rush into this. For now, you're just looking and thinking ahead.

Allow the wire to straighten out, and unlay the running end strands to the service. Bend the work into a loop again, and mark the spot on the standing part where the wire strand will enter. Let the wire straighten out once again, and clamp it into a vise with the unlayed strands pointing away from you. Apply superglue to the ends of the seven strands. Let the glue dry completely.

At the marked point, insert the marlinspike into the wire from left to right, as shown in the illustration. Take care to go over the heart and under three strands. If this is difficult, take a turn of the wire around your wrist. The space created as the strands unlay should be enough to insert the marlinspike. Rotate the marlinspike one full circle around the heart and down the wire (A). Leave the marlinspike in the wire.

Remove the work from the vise and loop it over a sturdy cup hook, door hinge pin—anything located at a comfortable working height that will hold.

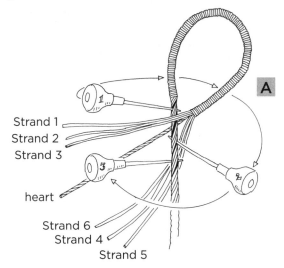

Strand 1
Strand 2
Strand 3
heart
Strand 6
Strand 4
Strand 5

Position Strand 1 at your mark on the standing part, and put on safety glasses. Maneuver the strand so it lies on top of the standing part, then turn it under and tuck it through the space

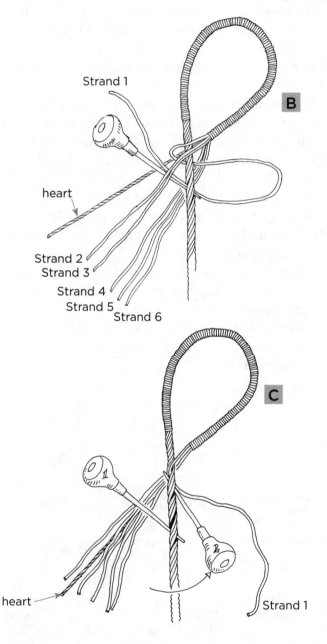

made by the spike. Roll the spike back and gently pull the slack out of the strand (B, C, and D). Tape or tie your work firmly so there is no gap where the ends of the service come together.

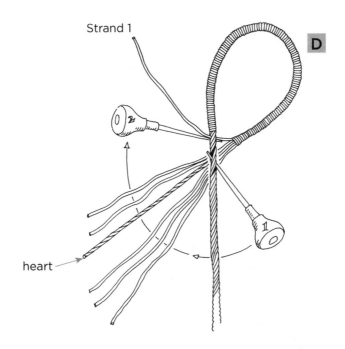

Strand 2 will enter the same opening but exit one strand farther from the eye. Lift two standing strands with the marlinspike this time, roll the marlinspike, tuck Strand 2, and roll the spike back (E).

Insert Strand 3 at the same opening as Strands 1 and 2. With the marlinspike, lift one standing strand and tuck Strand 3 (inset on E). To hold your work in place, tuck Strand 3 five more times under the same standing strand. As you tuck, wind the working strand (Strand 3) around the wire *with* the lay.

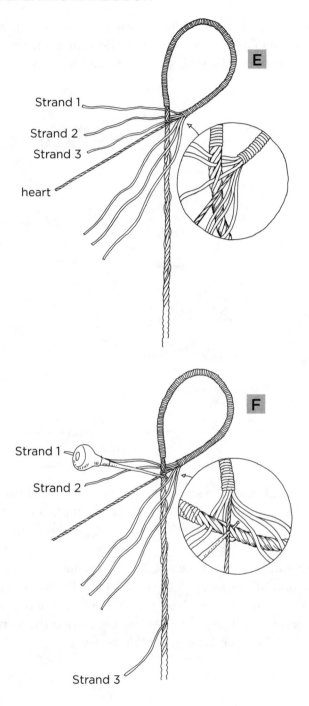

Strand 1

Strand 2

Strand 3

heart

E

Strand 1

Strand 2

Strand 3

F

To bury the heart, insert the marlinspike where Strand 3 was first tucked. Then set the heart across the wire and behind the spike. This motion or method is different from tucking. For lack of a better description, we're going to pry the heart into the center around the existing heart for several inches (G). You'll get the knack pretty quickly, because the wire will bind your tool if you're doing it incorrectly. Bury the heart for 6 inches (150 mm) and tape it to prevent the end from springing out.

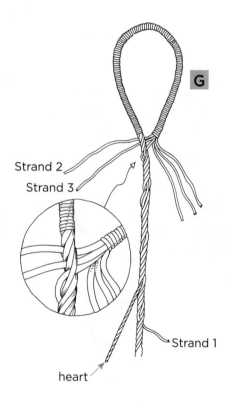

Insert the spike where the heart was inserted and lift one standing strand. Tuck Strand 4 six times the same way you tucked Strand 3. Repeat the process for Strands 5 and 6, tucking each under the same standing strand as Strand 4 (H). Then tuck Strands 1 and 2 each five more times. Clip the wire tails off close.

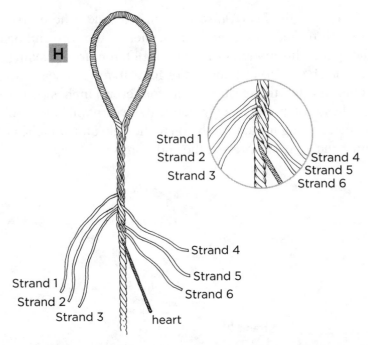

Strand 1
Strand 2
Strand 3

Strand 4
Strand 5
Strand 6

Strand 4

Strand 5

Strand 6

Strand 1
Strand 2
Strand 3

heart

Wrap the work with tarred electrical tape, starting from the bottom of the eye and working downward. Then apply the tarred nylon over the tape, against the lay of the wire, working from the base of the splice to the eye.

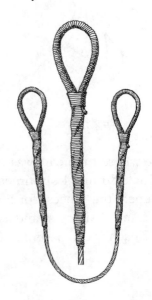

PART THREE

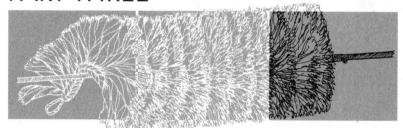

ROPEWORK
PROJECTS

TWENTY-ONE

Traditional Rope Fenders

Some items lend themselves well to people's ongoing attempts to upgrade them or make them more cost-efficient. I think synthetic manila rope, for example, still makes the grade. It's durable and chafe-resistant, fairly comfortable in hand, and impervious to rot. It's also inexpensive and has a nice, traditional look about it. The white plastic boat fenders that have replaced traditional manila rope fenders, however, score low. These plastic fenders are so light in weight that they will roll up and out from between the boat and the dock—or, much worse, from between two boats—resulting in dings, scuffed brightwork, and perhaps a few painfully pinched fingers. Yes, I'll grant that these bladder-style fenders are less expensive than a store-bought rope fender nowadays, but let's not forget that you can make a traditional rope fender inexpensively yourself.

We'll begin with a small rope fender measuring 10 inches (250 mm) long by 3 inches (75 mm) wide. I admit that this is a little on the small side, but it's easier to manage for a first-time fender builder, since the longer strands needed for larger fenders tangle more. For a larger fender, 12 inches (300 mm) long and 4 inches (100 mm) wide, follow these same directions, but use the amounts in parenthesis. Bigger fenders require larger rope and more of it.

TOOLS & MATERIALS

*21 feet (6.4 m) of ½-inch (12 mm)
manila rope (29 feet/8.8 m
of ¾-inch [19 mm] manila rope)*

*18 feet (5.5 m) of small stuff, such as
no. 21 tarred nylon (21 feet/6.4 m)*

Sharp knife

Vinyl tape

Swedish fid

*Small Swedish fid (a hollow fid of
U-shaped section that allows easy
"tucking" while splicing)*

Marking pen

If you'd like to make a white rope fender, I recommend using Wall's Poly Plus rope in the sizes specified above. Making a rope fender is also a good opportunity to recycle old rope.

Middle a 14-foot/4.3 m (20-foot/6 m) length of ½-inch/12 mm (¾-inch/19 mm) rope. Form an eye by wrapping tape around the doubled rope at 2½ inches/64 mm (3½ inches/90 mm) from the bight. Measuring carefully, cut eight pieces of filler rope to 9 inches/230 mm (11 inches/275 mm) long. Arrange the filler pieces around the doubled rope, just below the tape, and tie them on tightly—with twine and a constrictor knot, see opposite—to give bulk to the fender.

Unlay a few inches (75 mm) of the middle pieces that extend beyond the filler rope. Wrap the end of each of the six unlaid strands with tape to prevent them from unraveling. Continue unlaying the middle pieces all the way to the filler pieces. Make sure the bottom lashing on those filler pieces is about 1 inch (25 mm) from the ends and *tight*. A constrictor knot (shown in the illustration) works fine.

The following process will cover the cut ends of the filler ropes. Sit in a comfortable chair and firmly clamp the fender between your knees so the unlaid strands come toward you from the center of the fender. Arrange them so they are uniformly spaced and exit the fender in a fairly orderly fashion.

Select any strand (we'll call it Strand 1) and place it outside and under the strand to its immediate left (we'll call it Strand 2). Leave a loop in Strand 1, and give the two strands a good, tight twist, sending Strand 1 toward you (see art following pages).

Strand 2 should end up at the base of the strand to *its* left (Strand 3). Repeat the action described above, but do not leave a loop this time. Continue twisting pairs around the center until there is only the Strand 1 loop and one loose strand remaining (Strand 6). Slip Strand 6 up through the loop from the bottom, as shown.

Tighten the loop around Strand 6. Your work should look like a circular row of crown knots.

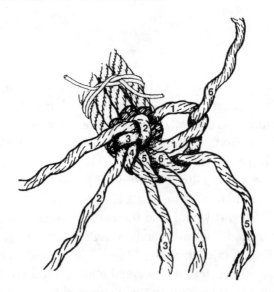

Knot another row of crown knots, taking care not to pull any one strand too tight, as it will cause your work to become distorted. By the time you start knotting the third row, you will have covered the ends of the fillers.

Continue knotting up the fender, covering the filler pieces. You may find the going easier if you lay the fender across your lap. By now, you will have discovered how quickly the strands tangle up. Tangles are an inherent part of the job, so have patience and keep going.

When you are an inch or two (25 to 50 mm) from the top, make sure the tape surrounding the base of the eye is entirely in view and that the tops of the filler ropes are evenly cut all the way around. Tailor the filler ropes, if necessary, by cutting down their tops and trimming their edges, as shown. This will produce a rounded top on the fender. Now replace the vinyl tape with a seizing of tarred nylon (see page 127 for instructions).

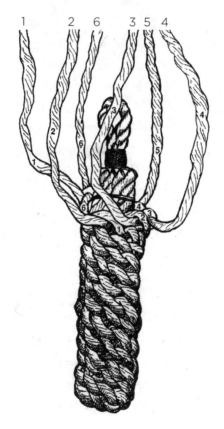

Continue knotting until the filler pieces are covered. To close up the top, you will use a modified version of the same knot. To start, separate the six strands into three pairs. Use the pairs to tie the knot just as before, but arrange it so the ends go through the loops from the top downward. Make the knot of three pairs tight.

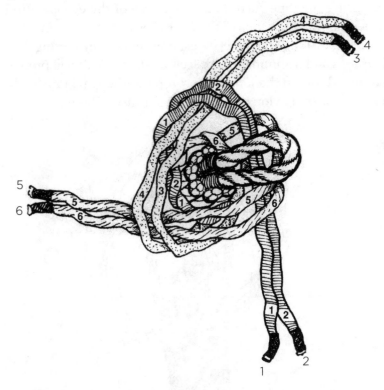

To finish the fender, tuck in the loose strands and cut them off. Using the Swedish fid, raise a bight in the last row you knotted. Run the strand that lies just above the bight through the fid. Pull it snug and remove the fid. Repeat this action again in the next row of knots below, tucking the same strand a second time. Then cut off the strand close to the side of the fender. Do the same with each of the live remaining loose strands.

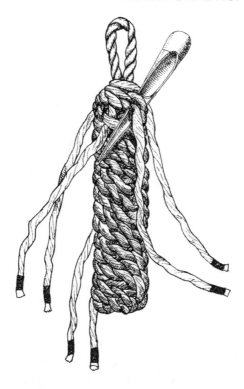

Your traditional rope fender is ready for use.

Dressing Up a Vinyl Fender

There's no question about it: Vinyl fenders are better than their predecessors, which were typically canvas sleeves filled with cork or kapok. Vinyl stays clean. It's light and strong. Its one drawback is aesthetic: Vinyl fenders shout, "I'm plastic!"

The method I've laid out below disguises the "plastic-ness" of vinyl fenders with a cotton duck cover and further dresses them with a neatly knotted and spliced lanyard. (The instructions are for Taylor's "Big B.")

TOOLS & MATERIALS

6 × 15 inches (150 x 380 mm) vinyl fender

42 inches (1070 mm) of ⅜-inch (9 mm) twisted nylon or Dacron line

Small Swedish fid

Scissors or a sharp knife

Hot knife or a flame source

Ruler

Waxed whipping twine and a needle

Marking pen

23 × 21 inches (580 x 530 mm) of #10 cotton duck canvas

Two shoelaces or similar cords of sufficient length to close the fender cover ends

If you don't have your own supplier of marine goodies or a favorite chandlery, and you want to avoid multiple stops to round up these items, you can do it all with one call or visit to West Marine—except for the canvas. For that, you'll need to go to a marine canvas shop or an art-supply store. For rope, I prefer ⅜-inch (9 mm) twisted nylon from New England Ropes. This well-made, heat-treated stuff behaves when you're trying to work with the fender tucked under one arm, wishing for a third hand or a skyhook.

Measure 9 inches (230 mm) from one end of the line. At that spot, apply a tight whipping (see page 125 for instructions). Cut off the melted end, and then gently unlay the line for a short distance and tape each of the three strand ends. Try to preserve the twist in each of the strands; the decorative knob knot that you'll be tying soon will be all the richer for it.

Continue unlaying the strands down to the whipping. Form a 1-inch (25 mm) eye and splice one round of tucks.

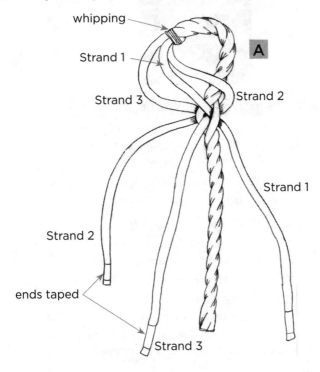

Holding your rope as shown in (B), tie a crown knot, counterclockwise. Turn the piece so the eye is pointing downward and tie another crown knot, this time clockwise. If you have trouble reversing the direction of the illustration while your line is inverted, tape a copy of it to your chest and stand in front of a mirror; this helps! Your knob knot is now complete—for the most part.

You need to double the knot in order to add richness and bulk. To do this, turn the piece over so the eye is facing up. Lay any strand along the same path as the one above it and to its right; tuck each strand twice. Repeat this for the remaining two strands and the knot will look like illustration C. You'll want to use the Swedish fid for this doubling procedure. The tool opens a smooth passage for the strands so that you won't find yourself fussing with snagged yarns.

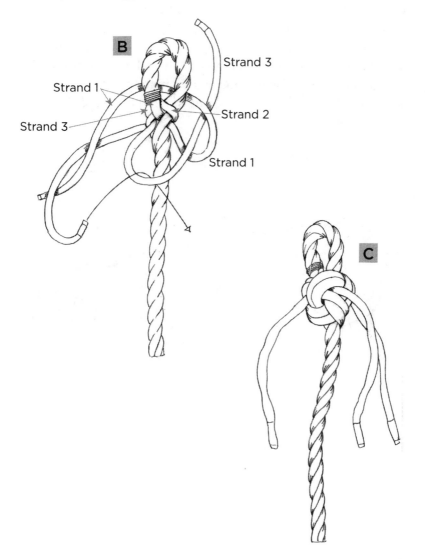

To finish the knot, you can simply cut off the ends and melt them. Better yet, you can thread each of the strands into the center of the knot and down, and splice in two more rounds of tucks.

With one end of the lanyard complete, lace it through the fender and tie the second knot. The process for the second knot is almost exactly like the first, but it's more awkward because the line is strung through the fender. The whipping for the second knot is applied to the line 4½ inches (112 mm) from the fender.

Sewing the canvas fender sleeve is pretty straightforward. First, fold the long edges over to form ¾-inch (19 mm) hems and stitch them, either on a machine or by hand. On the two ends, fold the material to form hems approximately 1 inch (25 mm) wide around each of the laces; again, stitch these either by hand or on a machine.

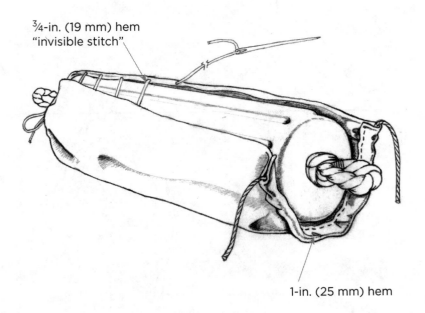

¾-in. (19 mm) hem "invisible stitch"

1-in. (25 mm) hem

Wrap the canvas cover around the fender and complete the job with needle, strong whipping twine, and the "invisible stitch," as shown in the illustration.

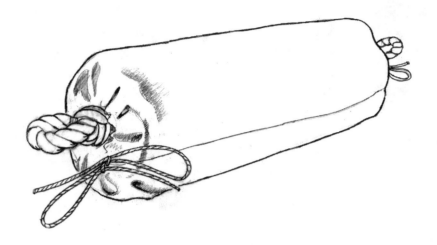

TWENTY-THREE

Bow Puddings

Bow puddings come in all shapes and sizes. The instructions below are for a 4 × 28-inch (100 × 710 mm) tapered, sausage-shaped fender, just right for the bow of your tender, skiff, or rowboat. On a tender, this "pudding" will protect the topsides of your larger boat when the tender's bow comes against it; but on any boat, a bow fender will save its own bow from bumps and dings.

Making this small pudding is fairly simple. Manila rope is knotted around a core of bundled polypropylene rope lengths, and eyes for attachment are fashioned at each end. You can also add a third eye around the girth of the fender in the center to help keep it from sagging after you've attached it. Larger fenders are often more elaborate. On tugboats you'll sometimes see a fluffy blanket installed over the top of a large pudding to keep it warm. No, not really. It's there to protect the pudding from chafe and to extend its life. The rope blanket, called a *collision mat*, is fastened to the fender and is covered with rope "whiskers," properly called *thrums*. When these thrums wear down, they're easily replaced, and the mat continues to protect the fender beneath it.

TOOLS & MATERIALS

30 feet (9 m) of ½-inch (12 mm) manila
19 feet (6 m) of small stuff,
such as #21 tarred nylon
32 feet (9.8 m) of ⅜-inch (9 mm)
polypropylene, preferably brown or black
¼-inch (6 mm) manila (optional)—5 feet
(1.5 m) for the third eye, 12 feet (3.7 m)
for a Turk's Head knot
Vinyl tape
Sharp knife or scissors
Small Swedish fid
Tape measure

Cut a 5 foot 9 inch (1.75 m) piece of the ½-inch (12 mm) manila and lay it out straight. At a spot 7 inches (175 mm) in from each end, tape or seize the rope tightly (see page 127 for seizing instructions). Unlay the rope to the tape or seizing. If the strands themselves want to unlay, tape their ends as well.

You'll splice the ends together to make an endless loop. If you simply stick the ends together and do the splice, you'll end up with a twist in your loop. To avoid this, arrange the rope as shown in the illustration on page 202. First, tie in the top loop; then, marry the ends, execute a short splice of two tucks, and taper the strands for the remaining tucks. Undo the tie that holds the closed loop, and you'll end up with a nice, round, endless loop.

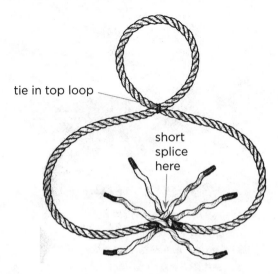

tie in top loop

short
splice
here

Make a couple of eyes so the fender can be attached to the boat. Collapse the loop with the splice in the center. At the two ends, form eyes that measure an inch (25 mm) or so. Seize them nicely with tarred nylon.

Cut 10 pieces of ⅜-inch (9 mm) polypropylene measuring 18 inches (450 mm) each. Polypropylene is the material of choice for the core, because it's less likely to rot than manila, it's lightweight, and it will bend more easily to conform to the shape of your bow. Parcel these lengths of polypropylene firmly around the ½-inch (12 mm) manila, at an even distance from each eye seizing.

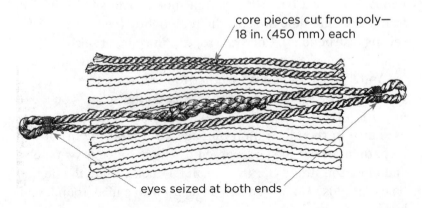

core pieces cut from poly—
18 in. (450 mm) each

eyes seized at both ends

Cut 17 more pieces of polypropylene, this time making them each 12 inches (300 mm) long. Tie them onto the core in another layer, as shown below. If you couldn't find black or brown polypropylene and bought brightly colored rope instead, you might want to parcel on a layer of manila fibers here (just a dusting of unlaid strands) to keep the color of your polypropylene from showing through the finished pudding.

core pieces cut from
poly—12 in. (300 mm)

At this stage of the game, you may want to consider an eye centered in the middle of the fender, protruding from the top of it. It is not critical on a fender of this size, but it's very handy on larger ones.

To make a centered eye, you'll need a 4-inch (100 mm) grommet. Unlay a single strand from the 5-foot (1.5 m) piece of ¼-inch (6 mm) manila. Middle the strand, form a 4-inch (100 mm) circle, and tie an overhand knot. Lay up the rope, and then

seizing

Grommet made from ¼-inch (6 mm) manila with a seizing tied in it to match eyes seized on ends of the pudding.

tuck the ends as you would for a long splice. Put a seizing on the grommet to match those on the other two eyes. Slip the grommet onto the fender and position it squarely in the center.

Next, you'll cover the polypropylene core you've just made with about a million hitches in manila. This part of the pudding takes the longest to do, but don't give up! The result is worth your patience.

Due to space limits, these illustrations won't show the rope strands at their full lengths.

Unlay a single strand from the 24-foot (7.3 m) length of ½-inch (12 mm) manila. Tape the ends of that strand, middle it, and set this point across the girth of the fender. Wrap one complete turn around the fender with one end of the strand, working outward from the middle. Do the same with the other end of the strand, going the other way from the middle.

If you made a centered eye, it will sit between the middle and left strands. Do not pull the work too tight.

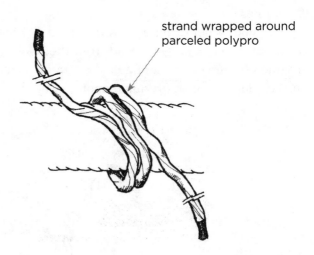

strand wrapped around parceled polypro

Start knotting the fender's coat. The proper name for this knotting is *needle hitching*. The first row of hitches is done a little differently from the rest: all of the hitches in this row are tied around both rope strands that encircle the girth of the fender.

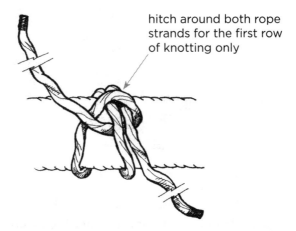

hitch around both rope
strands for the first row
of knotting only

Using your Swedish fid to make the work go easily, begin by
knotting (hitching) the strand on the left eight times up and over
the top; the strand on the right works for eight hitches down and
around the back (as shown in the illustration on next page).

strand on left works up

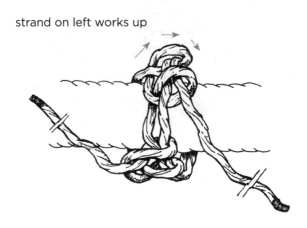

When these two strands are hitched eight times each around
the fender and meet again, the series of interlocking knots makes
an attractive, balanced design. (A larger fender will require more
than eight hitches, but for this size, eight is just right for the start
of a snug-fitting coat.)

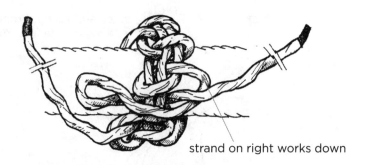

strand on right works down

Go back over your work and pull all the slack out, using your fid (see art below). You want the knotting to look snug and tidy, but don't strangle the fender or it will end up being too stiff.

For the next row of needle hitching, and for all the rows after that, lead the working end of one of the strands first down through a loop formed by the series in the first row, using your fid to open the loop, then up and out through its own bight (see art top of page 207). Continue making these new hitches, working each strand around the fender in opposite directions, toward opposite ends. (You can complete one end of the fender at a time.) Try to keep your hitches uniform and snug.

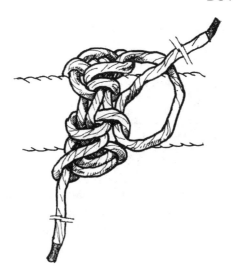

You'll need to add another strand when you start to run short. Unlay another single strand from the length of ½-inch (12 mm) manila. Run the end of the new strand under the work for a couple of rows and then out. When you're ready to begin working with the new strand, tuck the stubby end of the old strand under a tie and begin hitching with the new strand.

Continue knotting until you reach the drop-off at the end of the first layer of the poly core. You'll need to taper the manila layer of hitches to accommodate this change in shape and to keep the coat snug around the core. To do this, simply skip a loop. If the space that is left in the wake of this step seems too large, you skipped a space too soon. For this particular fender's coat, skip a loop just a bit after the place where the first layer

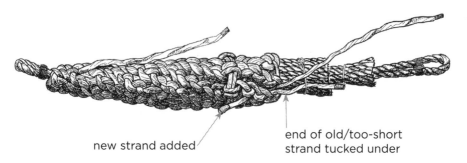

new strand added

end of old/too-short
strand tucked under

drops off. Then skip another just 1–1½ inches (25 to 38 mm) before the seized eye, just after the second layer ends.

To finish the pudding's coat in a tidy way, run the working end of the last strand back under the hitches for three rows. Bring it out and closely trim it and any other remaining strand ends. A Turk's Head knot (using ¼-inch/6 mm manila) tied at the center of the fender adds a nice, decorative touch. You'll find instructions for tying a Turk's Head knot in almost every book about knots.

Your fender will feel stiff, but you can make it flexible enough to bend around your boat's bow by tying a loop of rope through the two eyes and pulling it into a tight U shape overnight.

Turk's Head added
for decorative touch

TWENTY-FOUR

Baggywrinkle

If your mizzen is wearing thin where it chafes against the shrouds, or if a lazyjack is rubbing its way through that expensive mainsail, you need baggywrinkle (a cushion of natural rope yarns).

I won't jump into the debate about whether baggywrinkle is unsightly or fuzzy and cute. Yes, it looks like a big bottle brush—or maybe even one of those things from the car wash—but it also works, and a judicious application can save you major money at the sail loft. Baggywrinkle is best made from a natural rope yarn, so you can save otherwise useless lengths of slightly worn manila and recycle them into excellent raw material for the war on chafe. Baggywrinkle is meant to be sacrificial stuff; it wears down so your sails don't. For this reason, avoid using synthetic rope yarns, which turn from protectors to abraders.

Below are instructions for a baggywrinkle that will cover 1 foot (300 mm) of ³⁄₁₆-inch (5 mm) rigging.

> ### TOOLS & MATERIALS
>
> *12 feet (3.7 m) of ⅜-inch (9 mm) manila*
> *7 feet (2 m) of waxed #24 or #27 twine*
> *2–2½ feet (600 to 750 mm) of*
> *#21 tarred nylon for the seizing*
> *Vinyl tape*
> *Sharp knife*
> *Small Swedish fid (a hollow fid of*
> *U-shaped section that allows easy*
> *"tucking" while splicing)*
> *Marking pen*

Cut the manila into 6-inch (150 mm) lengths. Unlay all the pieces and, with your fingers, divide the separated strands in half. Middle the waxed twine, tie a tight Square Knot 1 inch (25 mm) from the bight, and set the loop on a strong hook.

Lay a half-strand of manila crosswise against the underside of the twine. Bring the ends of the manila around the twine and tuck them down through the middle to lock the knot. Slide the knot up the twine and lock it into place by jamming it tight. Add manila until this fringe is 38 inches (965 mm) long. Now might be a good time to settle in with a long playlist on your iPod.

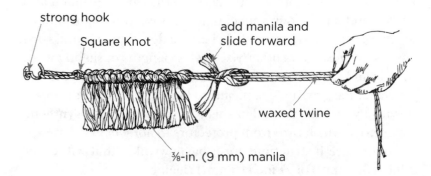

strong hook

Square Knot

add manila and
slide forward

waxed twine

⅜-in. (9 mm) manila

To affix the baggywrinkle to the wire rigging, seize the looped end to the wire with tarred nylon (seizing instructions are on page 127).

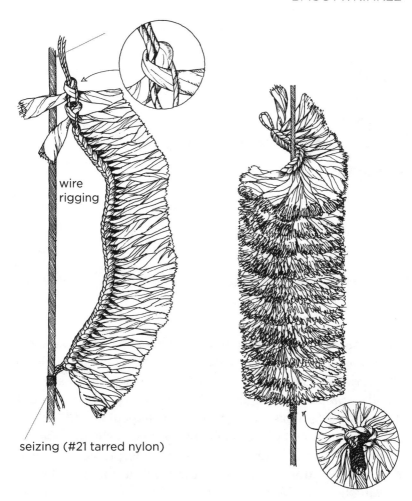

wire
rigging

seizing (#21 tarred nylon)

Wrap this fluffy thing firmly around the wire in a spiral, snugging up the wraps tightly and finally seizing the other end. Completing this last step is not as difficult as you might imagine—the manila and waxed twine set in place quite nicely. (Using electrical tape as bedding is unnecessary, and it will only serve to trap moisture.)

Once you have the knack, you can make baggywrinkle in any useful size, from about 6 inches (150 mm) to 2 feet (600 mm) in length. Now try to find out the origin of the word *baggywrinkle*.

TWENTY-FIVE

A Cargo Net

A cargo net is a handy item to have aboard. It allows the safe transfer of large, bulky items from the dock or tender to the deck of a larger boat. The following instructions are for a small but muscular cargo net. It measures 4 × 4 feet (1.2 × 1.2 m) with 6-inch-square (150 sq mm) openings. It's easy to stow and makes a bundle small enough to carry under one arm or fit without much fuss in a dory or tender; it will pay for its passage aboard larger ships. In the illustration, the laden net is being hoisted aboard the schooner *Ernestina* via the anchor

TOOLS & MATERIALS
23 feet (7.9 m) of ⅝-inch (16 mm) rope
168 feet (50.4 m) of ⅜-inch (9 mm) rope
30 feet (9 m) of tarred nylon twine (size #18 or #21)
Vinyl tape
Sharp knife
Small Swedish fid
Marking pen
Measuring tape or rule

burton. On a smaller boat, the net might hang from a block-and-tackle system made off to the boom.

Read through the instructions before you begin, and try to visualize the process. If you do this first, building the net will be much easier.

Cut 14 12-foot (3.7 m) lengths of ⅜-inch (9 mm) line. These pieces will serve as the body of the net. (Here's a hint: Tape the place where the rope is to be cut, then cut through the tape. This will keep the ends from unraveling.)

For the selvage (the perimeter of the net), you'll need the whole length of ⅝-inch (16 mm) line uncut. Take up the ⅝-inch (16 mm) piece and splice one of the 14 pieces of ⅜-inch (9 mm) rope into its center. This is a simple ring splice, except that the center strand runs through the selvage to keep it from sliding. The first and third strands simply run around the selvage.

On both sides of the center, splice in three more of the small pieces along the selvage (see art, below). One edge of the net is now complete, with seven pieces spliced into the selvage. (I'll call this the top edge, for the sake of these instructions.)

Now you will set in a couple of lifting eyes at the corners of the top edge. From the spot where the end piece of ⅜-inch (9 mm) line is spliced into the selvage, measure out 6 inches (150 mm) and put a mark on the selvage. Measure another 6 inches (150 mm) from this mark, and make another mark. Pinch the line together so the two marks meet.

To make the eye permanent, put a tight seizing where the marks meet (see page 127 for seizing instructions). Make a second eye at the other end.

To form the squares, splice another piece of ⅜-inch (9 mm) line to the left selvage, 6 inches (150 mm) below the eye. Splice in the six remaining strands at 6-inch (150 mm) intervals.

Next, use the Swedish fid to run the ⅜-inch (9 mm) strand located on the top edge nearest the left corner through the horizontal strand. It should enter 6 inches (150 mm) in from the selvage to create a 6-inch (150 mm) square.

Bend the horizontal piece around and insert the end through the vertical piece (see art below). This does two things: it locks the two pieces together, and it causes the directions of the two strands to change by 90 degrees. The vertical strand makes a sharp L turn and will now run horizontal, to the right. The horizontal strand takes a sharp turn and will now run vertical, downward (see art, top 218).

Form the next square by repeating the two-part locking step with the neighboring ⅜-inch (9 mm) piece. To keep the squares consistent, keep your ruler or tape close by—you'll want to check their sizes often. By now you'll have noticed that the strands are running in a stepwise pattern—over 6 inches (150 mm), down 6 inches (150 mm); over 6 inches (150 mm), down 6 inches (150 mm); and so on.

Finish locking in the squares from left to right. Tie up the body of the net by trimming and then splicing the ends into the right selvage. As you are doing this, be careful to keep the squares along the right edge a consistent 6-inch (150 mm) size.

The next step is to make two more small lifting eyes. As you did before, from the spot where the last ⅜-inch (9 mm) piece is spliced into the selvage, measure down 6 inches (150 mm) and mark the selvage. Measure another 6 inches (150 mm) and mark the selvage again.

Pinch the ⅝-inch (16 mm) rope together until the two marks meet, and tie a tight seizing to make the eye permanent. Put another eye in the other corner.

Trim the ends of the ⅝-inch (16 mm) selvage and "marry" them together. A long splice is a nice finishing touch here, but a

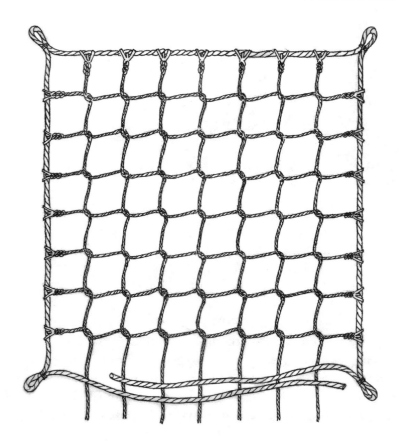

short splice (see page 30)—though not as invisible—will do just fine.

Trim and splice the seven remaining ⅜-inch (9 mm) ends into the bottom edge of the selvage. The area will be "soft" from being unlaid and laid up again, so use a little more care splicing here as you finish your cargo net.

You'll find there's progressively more scrap as you trim the ⅜-inch (9 mm) pieces from left to right and from top to bottom. I set these instructions up this way for the sake of simplicity— dealing with 14 pieces of line of varying lengths seems to overly complicate things. However, if you want, you can adjust the lengths of these lines in order to save material. Or you can do the project as outlined here and end up with a good collection of ever-handy "small stuff."

TWENTY-SIX

Making Your Own Rope

Rope designers use methods such as the following when working with a new fiber or yarn to get a feel for how much material is needed to make a specific rope and how much it will need to be twisted during manufacture. Many thousands of feet of rope have been sold from displays of short samples made this way.

TOOLS & MATERIALS
Twine (at least 10 feet/3 m)
Scissors or sharp knife
Wooden pencil
Vinyl tape

If you are using nylon twine, tape the ends to prevent unlaying. Tie one end of the twine to a fixed hook. Holding the pencil horizontally about 3 feet (915 mm) from the hook, alternately pass the twine around the pencil and hook until you have made at least 1½ complete rounds, the equivalent of three rope yarns. The diameter of the twine and the number of rope yarns formed will determine the diameter of the strand of rope you are making. This strand will be one-half the diameter of the finished three-strand rope, although you will triple your worked piece after the initial twisting.

When you have three or more yarns, tie off the unsecured end to the pencil or hook. Pull on the pencil to impose a uniform tension and length on the yarns.

Lightly grasp the bundle of yarns in the fist of your left hand with the pencil resting outside your thumb and forefinger. The tube formed by your fist is similar to a ropemaker's strand tube.

While keeping tension on the bundle of rope yarns with your fist, turn the pencil clockwise with the index finger of your right hand to form the rope strand. The number of twists you put into the strand will determine the firmness of the finished rope. You should stop twisting before the rope kinks; if it does kink, just turn the pencil counterclockwise until the kink disappears.

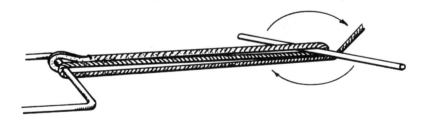

Grasp the pencil with your right hand and keep tension on the strand throughout this step. With two fingers of your left hand, grasp the strand midway between the pencil and the hook, forming a bight. Pass the pencil behind the hook and back again, inserting it through the bight of strand in your left hand. Don't let the strand go slack.

You now have three parallel and highly twisted strands. Grasp them with a fist as before, and twist the pencil counterclockwise until it stops. The finished rope won't unlay of its own accord. Ropemakers refer to this characteristic as balance.

Tape the rope just shy of each end and cut off the ends. You now should have a short piece of three-strand rope that looks as though it was cut as a sample from a large spool of machine-made rope.

TWENTY-SEVEN

Quick and Easy Knots

Piecing together rope and placing eyes, or loops, at the end of rope require splices that offer a high degree of safety, strength, and dependability. The knots in this chapter, however, serve best in those light-duty situations not requiring the exceptional strength of a well-constructed splice. It is important to remember that the working load of a rope can be reduced by as much as half when it is knotted.

Among the 19 knots in this chapter are the 17 a sailor must master in order to become a licensed Able-Bodied Seaman in the U.S. Merchant Marine (the outriders are the Package Knot and the Fisherman's Knot). In recent years, I've been teaching at the New England Maritime Institute, one of a handful of such schools that appeared around the country in the wake of the Exxon *Valdez* disaster. Consistency and safety are the prime directives. The U.S. Coast Guard requires each licensed mariner to know these knots by heart.

The first pair of knots belong to the group known as stopper knots because their function is to stop a rope from slipping through a block, clutch, or other hardware. The simplest stopper knot is the lowly but useful Overhand Knot. Add another twist and you get the bulkier and therefore more useful Figure-Eight Knot.

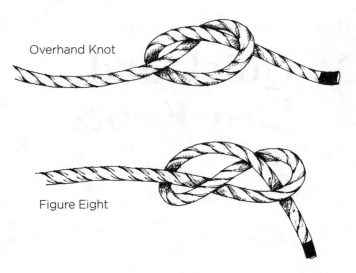

Overhand Knot

Figure Eight

Hitches are used to secure the end of a line to an object, either to move the object or to belay the line and keep it from moving. The Clove Hitch is a versatile, quick-to-tie choice for

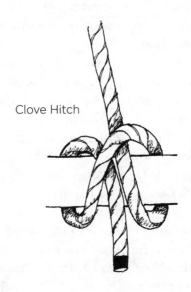

Clove Hitch

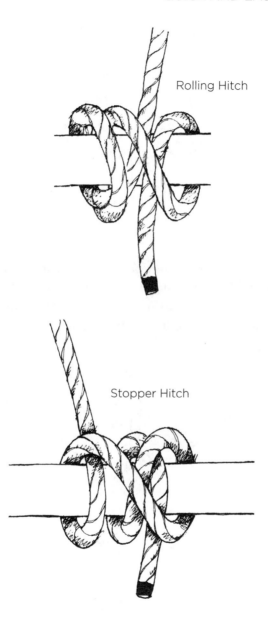

Rolling Hitch

Stopper Hitch

light and temporary duty, but the Rolling Hitch provides an added measure of security. The Stopper Hitch is especially effective for a super grip—say, when towing a timber through the water or dragging it across land.

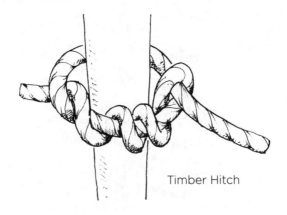

Timber Hitch

If the stopper hitch fails you, try the Timber Hitch, a great choice for picking up a long, round timber or spar. But if it's a bucket or barrel you're lifting, you won't find a simpler, more effective knot than the Barrel Hitch finished off with a Bowline (see below).

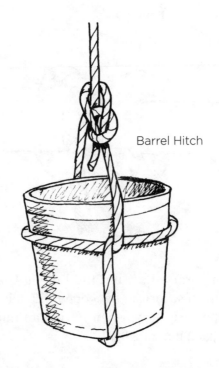

Barrel Hitch

Returning from the exotic to the mainstream, the Two Round Turns with Two Half Hitches has a self-explanatory name if there ever was one. This is a good, secure belay for the end of any line. And let's not forget the Anchor Bend, which, despite its name, is really another hitch. Tie it through the ring of your anchor and rest easy, especially if you take the trouble to seize the end to the standing part.

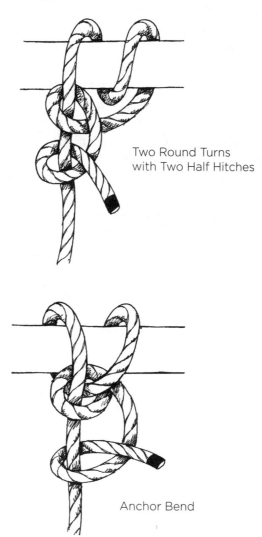

Two Round Turns
with Two Half Hitches

Anchor Bend

Bowline

A mariner finds many needs for a loop in the end of a line, to slip over something or to tie around something. Docklines, towlines, painters, lashing lines—many is the line that spends some portion of its working life sporting a loop in one or both ends. For a permanent loop, nothing beats an Eye Splice, but for a temporary loop, the Bowline (above) is a workhorse of a knot. There are many methods for tying it—all of them easy—and it's just as easy to untie. A Bowline on a Bight (opposite) is a good choice when you require two loops that will be subjected to approximately equal tension in the same direction. It works well as a bosun's chair.

The French Bowline, properly tied, produces an excellent rescue sling. The two loops adjust automatically to the parts of

French Bowline

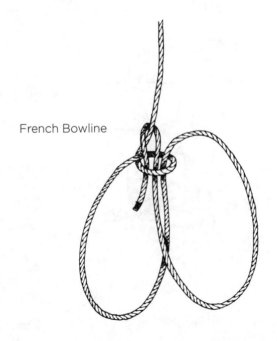

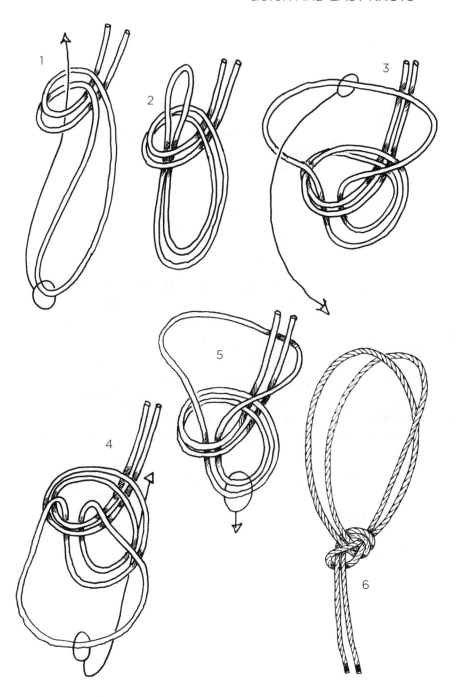

Bowline on a Bight

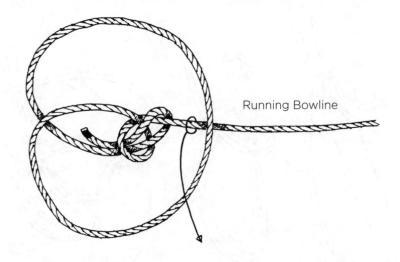

Running Bowline

the body they encircle. The Running Bowline produces a slip knot that is relatively easy to untie. To tie it in a heavy dockline or hawser, one end of which is already belayed, make the small loop (i.e., the "rabbit's hole"), then "frame" the knot with a big loop, as shown. Pass the end under the beginning of the big loop, then back up through the small loop, behind the standing part; then down through the small loop again as for an ordinary bowline. Now, when you pull a bight of the standing part up through the big loop, you'll have your slip-knotted loop to drop over a bitt or bollard (1).

The Cat's Paw is a simple but elegant knot designed to reduce the chances of a heavy load slipping off the hook of a block and tackle. Twist the loops as shown into the sling holding the cargo, then drop the loops over the hook. It won't jam, and it will spill instantly when removed from the hook.

Cat's Paw

A bend is called for when the time comes to tie two ends of rope together. The most common bend, although not the best, is the Square Knot, or Reef Knot. A square knot should not slip if it is tied with two ends of the same size, but it can lock under tension, making it difficult to untie. The square knot usually should not be used to join two pieces of rope except as a temporary expedient because it is not particularly secure and will capsize easily if rubbed the wrong way by, say, a shroud or bobstay. It's the knot of choice for tying reef points under the bunt of a reefed sail—thus, the alternate name. Tied wrong, this knot becomes a Granny Knot and is more likely to slip.

Square Knot

The Package Knot is simply a square knot with an extra turn in the first overhand. It is a good alternative to the square knot because it is easier to untie. It does not hold as well, however.

Package Knot

The Fisherman's Knot is strong and easy to tie, but untying it is very difficult. (In the illustration, the knot has not yet been cinched tight.)

Fisherman's Knot

The Sheet Bend is much easier to untie than a square knot after it has been under strain, and is an excellent choice to join ropes of different sizes. When a ship is docking, for example, the smaller line is thrown onto the ship from the dock and is then tied with a single (or double) sheet bend onto the ship's dockline (often wire). Then the dockline is hauled over to the dock and belayed. When one of the lines already has an eye in it, the knot is called a Becket Bend. It is important to pull the knot tight so the loops seat firmly with like ends parallel to each other. If this bend is not drawn tight properly, the two pieces can slip.

Sheet Bend

Towing hawsers can be joined with a Carrick Bend. If the ends are not seized onto the standing part of the rope, however, the knot can seize under strain and be difficult to untie.

Carrick Bend

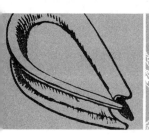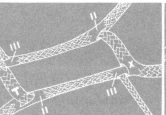

GLOSSARY

aircraft cables Strands, cords, and wire ropes made of special-strength wire primarily for aircraft controls and miscellaneous uses in the aircraft industry.

anchor cable Chain, line, wire, or a combination of them used to attach a vessel to its anchor.

ASTM International Originally known as the American Society of Testing and Materials. Publishes many standards on the subjects of wire rope design and manufacture and the materials used to make it.

belay To secure a rope with turns around a cleat or bit.

bend Knot used to join two ropes.

bight A loop in a length of chain or rope.

bitt Wood or iron post on a deck for securing mooring lines or towlines.

bitter end The nonworking end of a line or chain.

bollard Iron mooring post on a pier.

breaking strength Load required to break a synthetic or wire rope under tension.

cable A term loosely applied to wire ropes, wire strands, and electrical conductors.

cable clamp A style of hardware that consists of a threaded U-bolt and saddle.

chafe To wear or fray a rope.

clew The lower after corner of a fore-and-aft sail.

coat The outer covering of two-part rope.

coil Neat circles of rope, line, or chain piled to keep the loops free of tangles.

construction Refers to the design of wire rope, including number of strands, number of wires per strand, and the arrangement of wires in each strand.

cord Refers to small sizes of wire ropes.

cordage Rope or ropelike material varying in size from twine to hawser; in nautical handiwork, rope of less than ½ inch (12 mm) diameter, or small stuff.

core The inner section of two-part rope; the member of a wire rope about which the strands are laid. The member may be fiber, a wire strand, or an independent wire rope.

corrosion The chemical decomposition of the wires of a rope by exposure to moisture, acids, alkalines, or other destructive agents.

diameter The distance measured through the center of a cross section of synthetic or wire rope. For noncritical use, determine the diameter by measuring the rope's circumference, or girth, and divide by 3.

eye A loop spliced at the end of a synthetic or wire rope.

fake A circular pile of rope; it is organized and on one plane. A Flemish coil.

fid A splicing tool used to guide the rope strand into place.

galvanize To coat with zinc to protect against corrosion.

galvanized wire Wire coated with zinc.

guard rail cable A galvanized wire rope erected along a highway.

guy line A wire strand or rope, usually galvanized, for holding a structure in position.

halyard Any rope or wire used to hoist sails.

hardness A measure of the force required to open the strand of a rope. A hard rope almost stands by itself.

hawsepipe Metal tube that allows passage of the anchor cable to the chain locker.

hawser Towline or mooring line more than 5 inches (13 cm) in circumference.

heart The center strand or core of a wire rope, of layed wire, or lubricated wire.

heaver A handmade tool used to apply service.

hitch Knot used to tie a line to a hook, ring, or spar.

hockle A condition whereby a rope strand twists on itself; also called a *chinkle.*

independent wire rope core Wire rope used as the core of a larger rope.

jury rig Make or fix using ingenuity and whatever materials are at hand.

kink A tight hockle that upsets the lay of a synthetic rope; a sharp bend in a wire rope that permanently distorts the wires and strands.

knot A weak substitute for a splice, but easy to unfasten.

lanyard A length of small stuff, sometimes decorative, tied to an object to make it secure.

lash To secure with rope.

lay The direction of the twist in a synthetic rope strand (see right-laid); the manner in which wires are helically laid into strands or strands into rope (see right-laid).

line Rope with a specific use.

make fast To secure a rope.

marl A form of seizing.

marline Two-strand, left-laid, tarred hemp.

marlinspike Tapered steel tool used to separate strands in a wire rope during splicing.

marry To interlace two ropes, end to end, for splicing.

mooring lines Rope used to tie a boat to a wharf or pier.

mousing Seizing used to prevent a pin from unscrewing and falling out of the shackle or to close the opening of a hook.

preformed wire rope Wire rope in which the strands are permanently shaped, before fabrication into the rope, to the helical form they assume in the wire rope.

pick On the surface of a braided rope, the visible yarn between the emergence from and the exit to the inside of the braided rope.

picks per inch (ppi) The number of parallel picks in 1 inch (2.5 cm) of braided rope. The picks per inch, selected at manufacture, determine strength and flexibility of the braided rope.

preventer A length of wire chain or line that acts as a safeguard or backup tether to keep an object (e.g., a boom) from moving unexpectedly.

reeve To pass the end of a rope through a hole.

rigging Any assembly made from wire rope that is to be used for lifting, pulling, holding, or strapping capacity; wire rope or aircraft cable used for securing the mast or boom of a sailboat and for the running of sails.

right-laid Rope with strands twisted up and to the right when the end points away from the viewer.

seize To securely bind the end of a wire rope or strand with seizing wire or strand.

seizing strand Small strand, usually of seven wires made of soft annealed wire.

seizing wire Soft annealed wire.

serve To cover the surface of a line or wire with a smooth wrapping of fiber cord.

serving mallet A hammerlike tool used to apply wrapping turns around a line or splice.

small stuff Rope of less than ½ inch (12 mm) diameter.

splice The interweaving of two ends of ropes so as to make a continuous or endless length without appreciably increasing the diameter; making a loop, or an eye, in the end of a rope by tucking the ends of the strands.

stainless steel rope Wire rope made of chrome-nickel steel wires having great resistance to corrosion.

standing part The area in the rope that is inactive, as opposed to the working end, bitter end, or bight.

strand An arrangement of fibers or wires helically laid about an axis or another fiber or wire center to produce a symmetrical section.

surge Let the strain off a line intermittently, in a controlled fashion.

swaged fittings Fittings in which wire rope is inserted and attached by a cold-flowing method.

tackle A system of lines and blocks to gain additional lifting or pulling power.

take a turn Run a line around a cleat or bitts.

taper To diminish the diameter of a rope smoothly by selectively removing strands or yarns.

thimble A grooved ring made of plastic or metal that fits tightly inside an eye splice.

tiller rope/cable A very flexible operating rope, commonly made by cable laying six 6 × 7 ropes around a fiber core resulting in a 6 × 42 construction; a $\frac{3}{32}$-inch (2mm) 7 × 7 galvanized cable coated to an outside diameter of $\frac{3}{16}$ inch (5mm) with vinyl or nylon.

tuck To push a single strand through the body of a rope (fiber or wire).

turnbuckle A device attached to wire rope for making limited adjustments in length. It consists of a barrel and right- and left-hand threaded bolts.

twine Rope of a diameter larger than a sewing thread but smaller than a shoelace.

unlay To take the twist out of a three-strand rope. The ends of the three strands are taped to prevent them from unlaying.

vang A tackle positioned on the vessel to prevent the boom from raising.

whip Wrap the end of rope with small stuff to prevent the rope from unlaying.

wire rope A plurality of strands laid helically around an axis or a core.

working load A manufacturer's recommendation of the maximum pounds of pull to which a rope can safely be subjected; generally, one-tenth the new rope's breaking strength.

working part The end of the rope you are using to make a splice (compare with standing part).

yarn A group of fibers twisted together; thread.

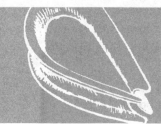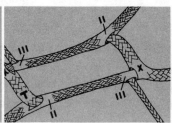

INDEX